Feng Shui

A Layman's Guide to Chinese Geomancy

Evelyn Lip

平安国际出版社
HEIAN INTERNATIONAL, INC.

by Evelyn Lip

© Illustrations: Evelyn Lip
© 1979 Times Editions Pte Ltd, Singapore

First American Edition 1987
Fifth American Edition 1996

HEIAN INTERNATIONAL, INC.
Publishers
1815 W. 205th Street, Suite 301
Torrance, CA 90501

ISBN 0-89346-286-1

Printed in Malaysia

Note on Romanization

The romanization of Chinese terms and names of people or buildings has been at times difficult because, strictly speaking, it should follow the Mandarin pronunciation. But if this were so, it would render some of the famous buildings unfamiliar as they have been called in their particular dialect since their erection. For example, the well-known Giok Hong Tian (玉皇殿) at Havelock Road, Singapore, romanized in Hokkien pronunciation, would become *Yu Huang Dian* in Mandarin. Thus it has been decided that spellings of names and terms are to appear in accordance with historical records and traditional practice. In cases where they have not been traditionally established, the romanization according to Mandarin pronunciation is used.

Contents

Foreword by Professor E.J. Seow

There are many approaches to architecture from the functional to the intangible. Architects differ in their approaches and if architecture is the art of creating the living environment, then the approaches are limitless.

As one who has practised architecture for many years, I have frequently experienced *feng shui* through the agency of benign and knowledgeable clients who have successfully and constantly followed its precepts. In the world of Chinese Design Methods, whether building at a T-junction, at the foot of a hill or on a triangular site, a set of rules, as stringent as normal municipal building bylaws, have to be conformed with.

From *feng* (wind) to *shui* (water) one discerns the gaseous elements of the environment (air, wind, ventilation, airconditioning) or its liquid aspects (rain, drainage, sanitation, dampness, waterproofing, rain-protection)—all within the ambit of normal solid architectural practice. Lao Tze the philosopher had suggested that the reality of a building does not consist in four walls and a roof, but in the space enclosed.

I suggested to Evelyn Lip that she might look into the mass of information on the topic and perhaps suggest a guide for tyro architects and others on these intangible things which form a ponderable part of solid state architecture with or without architects. I wish her success in her search for meanings, and I am sure—like acupuncture, bird's nest and sharksfin—it will create interest and provide food for thought in these seemingly imponderable things.

Professor E.J. Seow
Head
School of Architecture

29 March 1979

Preface

The chief literary sources on geomancy or *feng shui* available locally are contained in a number of books. However, none of them attempt to explain how one reads the *feng shui* of a building or a site using a *luopan* or geomancer's compass.

In Singapore and Malaysia, the art of divining by the reading of the *luopan* is a closely guarded secret and it costs a curious inquirer or firm believer in geomancy at least $200 to $300 to consult a geomancer on the orientation of a building or tombstone. It is most astonishing to learn that many building developers and house owners seek advice from geomancers the moment they receive a set of architectural plans from their architects. Quite often the designers are more than puzzled when asked to re-orientate the building or re-position the doors or staircases for no obvious reason. It is rather awkward when an architect finds himself or herself in such a situation and has never heard of the practice and theory of feng shui.

Struck by the immense interest and the lack of any comprehensive compilation of this fascinating subject of Chinese pseudo-science, I ventured to carry out research and write a concise book. Quotations are taken from academic sources to establish the origin of geomancy, and an analysis of a few *luopan* is made so that what they contain can be presented with clarity.

The objectives of this book can be summarized briefly as follows: (1) to explain feng shui; (2) to present a collection of historical records and "rules-of-thumb" governing geomancy; and (3) to reveal a few examples of the *luopan*. It is hoped that by understanding the mysteries and philosophies of the myths that shroud this ancient Chinese art of divination, the reader will be able to distinguish the practical aspects from the superstitious and symbolic implications.

Acknowledgements

I am much indebted to Professor E.J. Seow, former head of the Department of Architecture, Faculty of Architecture and Building of the University of Singapore, for his kind suggestion and encouragement that I should carry out research on this very interesting topic. I am also indebted to Francis, my husband, who has given me constant and unceasing encouragement. My gratitude goes to the Editorial Board of the Singapore Institute of Architects Journal for allowing me to quote a paragraph from the article I contributed to its Journal (July/August 1978 issue) entitled *"Feng shui,* Chinese colours and symbolism"*. I am grateful to Miss Lee May Chu, former publisher of *Development and Construction,* for allowing me to quote an article I contributed to her magazine *Geomancy and Building* in 1977.

I am indebted to many people and organizations who have given me permission to use photographs and to give descriptions of their buildings related to *feng shui* practices.

The system of feng shui *is made up of the breaths of nature as well as the mathe-* ▶
matical forms of nature.

Introduction

Geomancy is defined as the art of divining the future for good or ill fortune, from the figure suggested by dots or lines placed at random on the earth's surface. It has been said that the fortunes of men depend on how well their ancestors were buried with respect to geomancy and also on how correctly their own dwellings were built with respect to orientation, planning, construction, etc. according to *feng shui* (风水) or geomancy. The words *feng shui* in Chinese mean the wind and the water. Actually *feng shui* is related to all the geographical features of the area in which a tomb is situated and in many aspects is connected with building and architectural features. It stands for the power of the natural environment—the wind and the air of the mountains and hills; the streams and the rain; and the composite influences of the natural processes.

Feng shui originated in China a few thousand years ago, spread to Japan and was adopted and used for the orientation of the imperial palaces. In traditional China, the concept of the location of buildings and dwelling units had great importance. There must be a prescribed siting, dimensioning and orientation of a town or even a dwelling. To the north the site should be hilly or have a mountainous shield to ward off evil influences. The dead should be buried on a south-facing slope as it receives the summer sun. The front of a site should preferably face the south. It should always have an unhindered view which would include a stream or the sea. The back of a site should always be the north and should be blocked. Left then should be the east and right the west.

This art of divination later spread further south to countries like Malaysia and Singapore. It is not known how much *feng shui* is still being practised in China nowadays. In modern Singapore and Malaysia it is still regarded as a guide to good fortune by some building developers and many house owners. The computation and derivation of correct orientation of buildings and tombs according to geomantic theories is still a very closely guarded art and is only known to experts who have been in this field for many years.

Historical Background

Evidence shows that as far back as three thousand years ago government residences and imperial palaces were built according to the theories of *feng shui*. Such evidence is found in ancient Chinese books, e.g. " 太保朝于洛卜宅，厥既得卜，则经营". This when translated means that the government officers on arrival at a city used the geomancer's compass to assess the site before the commencement of the construction of the buildings. The ancient books also mentioned that even well-educated men believed in divining the future through geomancy by the choice of burial tombs and burial dates (大夫卜宅与葬日). The art of geomancy became a professional skill during the Han dynasty and the *feng shui* specialists are called *kan-yu jia* (堪兴家). The words *kan-yu* are related to geographical and astronomical studies using astronomy and geographical conditions as bases to predict the good and bad omens of events. Sometimes the *kan-yu jia* are referred to as *di-li jia* (地理家). *Di-li* means geography.

Feng shui can also be considered a pseudophysical science of climatology and geomorphology. It resulted as a means to avoid winds from the north, devastating typhoons, thunderstorms, floods, droughts, and other forces of nature which affected the ancient Chinese. It could have been derived from the admiration of the work of nature which, through its agents of erosion, wind and water, has moulded the mountains, hills and valleys which form the greater portion of the land of China. The ancient Chinese, mostly agri-culturalists, had to rely on the wind and rain for their crops and became convinced they were controlled by nature. It appeared they had to behave according to its laws and orders.

Wu Wei, the Ming dynasty writer, summarizes the history of the develop-ment of geomancy as follows:

> The theories of the geomancers have their sources in the ancient *yin-yang* school.
>
> Although the ancients in establishing their cities and erecting their buildings always selected the site [geomanti-cally] the art of selecting burial sites originated with the Burial Book . . .

1 What is Geomancy or Feng Shui?

The ancient practice of geomancy is not only a means of divination, but also a logical way of foretelling the future based on external phenomena. According to the geomancer, if the ancestral burial ground is of "good" condition, the future generations would enjoy great fortune and good health. An illustration of this phenomenon was quoted by the author of *The Secret Theory of Geomancy* who related how Zhu Yuan Zhang (朱元璋) succeeded in becoming the first Emperor of the Ming Dynasty soon after his fisherman father buried his grandfather at a site known as the Cave for the King.

To the ancient Chinese death was relative to life and was considered an extension of living. They also held the belief that everything in the universe was intimately related. In fact, several other mystical philosophies believe that every movement in the universe gives rise to a reciprocal movement. For example, the principle of mathematical relationship found in Babylonian and Egyptian astrology and Indian philosophy holds the belief that motion and change are the alternating energies that control breathing. These beliefs are basic to the geomantic philosophy. Thus, man could only overcome his limitations by uniting all the energies or forces of nature with that of the Superior Being and harmonizing the flux of *yin* (阴) and *yang* (阳).

Different authors define geomancy differently but the basic meaning remains the same. *The Encyclopedia Sinica* gives the following definition: "*Feng shui*—wind and water, the outward and visible signs of celestial *yang* and *yin*; the art of adapting the residence of the living and the dead so as to harmonize with the cosmic breath." Lai Chuen Yan tells us that *feng shui* is a mystical combination of Chinese philosophical, religious, astrological, cosmological, mathematical and geographical concepts.[1] It is a unique dogmatic faith or superstition of the Chinese mind. E.J. Eitel[2] equates *feng shui* to the rudiments of Chinese natural science while L.C. Porter[3] interprets it as the art of keeping in time with nature. Joseph Needham has this to say of *feng shui*:[4] "The forms of hills and the directions of water courses, being the outcome of the moulding influences of winds and waters . . ." It is beyond the scope of this study to explain in detail the link between geomancy and the burial of the dead. However, a brief introduction to this idea would be useful at this juncture.

[1]   Lai Chuen Yan, "A Feng Shui Model as a Location Index", *Annals of the Association of American Geographers,* Vol. 64, No. 4.
[2]   E.J. Eitel, *The Rudiments of Natural Science in China* (Hong Kong, 1873).
[3]   L.C. Porter, "How the Chinese Keep in Time with Nature", *Chinese Recorder,* Vol. 51, 1920, pp. 837-50.
[4]   Joseph Needham, *Science and Civilization in China,* London, 1943.

Five factors govern the choice of a burial place or building site. These are as follows:

龙	*long*	:	dragon. This represents the location of the burial ground.
穴	*xue*	:	hole, but in geomancy it indicates the foundation of the tomb or building site.
砂	*sha*	:	it symbolizes the surroundings or neighbouring environment of the site.
水	*shui*	:	water. It depicts the streams flowing through or bypassing the site.
向	*xiang*	:	the orientation or the direction of the site.

All these factors have to be seriously considered when choosing a burial place or building site. Once they have been decided they will influence the future or fate of the people involved.

To the geomancer, the dragon is the most significant factor as it either makes or destroys the fortune of man. Hence it is the symbol of the beneficial forces of nature and the Superior Being. The advance and retreat of the dragon form the basis of the *Yi-Jing*[5] principle. In geomancy, the "twists and turns" or the "ups and downs" of the body of the dragon represent the topography of the site. A "false" dragon (假龙) means that the land is flat while a "real" dragon has a good undulating profile. This "good" profile ensures that the site is favourable and is of solid ground. Besides determining the favourability of the profile of the dragon (i.e. favourability of the location of the site of the tomb), the geomancer is also able to determine the kind of dragon that exists on the site: whether it is a "straight" dragon (直龙), a dragon lying across the site (横龙) or a dragon riding on the site (骑龙).

[5]   *Yi-Jing* is the *Book of Changes* and was one of those few books that escaped the destruction of all the books in China ordered by Chin Shih Huang Ti in 213 B.C. It is a book of prophecies often referred to by the Chinese and is based on the principles of the duality of *yin* and *yang*. *Yi-Jing* offers predictions about the world in flux and the forces which constantly change life. A translation by James Legge, edited by Raymond van Over, was published by New American Library, New York, in 1971.

The burial ground must not only have the profile of a good dragon but also the "breath of cosmic life". (The Chinese believe that a dead and buried person must have "air to breathe". If this air is good it is called *sen chi* (生气) or the "breath of cosmic life". A lack of cosmic breath would affect the well-being of the dead and the fortune of his descendants!) Land that is flat, waterlogged or not backed by a hill is considered unsuitable.

The *xue* or foundation factor is the most difficult to assess. There is a saying, "To find the dragon is easy, the *xue* difficult." In the ancient *Song of Geomancy*[6] there is a line which tells us that it takes three years to find the dragon but ten years to find the *xue* (三年寻龙，十年点穴). This proves that even with experience and knowledge, the geomancer finds it a difficult task to assess the *xue* of a site.

There are three types of *sha* or sand which the geomancer looks for. These are represented by the various "star" symbols. The Star of Fire represents sand that has a sharp and cutting edge while the Star of Wood is sand that is round and straight. Sand that is long and round is called the Star of Gold, whilst sand that forms a wave-like pattern is called the Star of Earth. Once the quality of the sand has been determined and classified accordingly, the divination of the site can then be computed, e.g. sand that is round, regular and full is reputed to bring fortune, while sand that is irregular and defective is supposed to spell bad fortune. In a Chinese book on geomancy, as many as twenty-seven types of sand are described in detail.

Both *shui* and *xiang* (water and orientation respectively) are essential features in the houses of the living as well as the dead. According to the geomancer, the buried need fresh air. Without wind, the air is still; with wind, the air circulates.

---

6   *Song of Geomancy,* written by Kuo P'u in the 4th century B.C., gives burial rules and makes geomantic comments. It comes in twenty parts. Kuo P'u was a **scholar**, poet and master of occult arts.

◄

Tomb orientation. It is believed that the soul continues to live after death in the spirit world, thus graves are the yin *habitations as distinct from that of the living. Tombs and buildings are supposed to be built where the* feng shui *is most favourable. Their siting is seen as a means of establishing and maintaining good fortune. The south-facing slope is preferred for a burial ground as it is considered to be with "life and cosmic breath". According to the* New Nation *(13 February 1978), geomancers in Hong Kong spent considerable time looking for a good site to bury the dead. Finally a small island in Miro Bay was chosen even though it meant inconvenience to devotees as they had to travel through a restricted zone to visit a grave. To the geomancers a site with "cosmic breath" is vital to the burial ground.*

The quality of *shui* is believed to be divided into good or bad. Slow-moving water around the house or burial ground is generally believed to bring good luck. To get an accurate assessment of the entire external environment is necessary because the location, ground and quality of the sand do in fact affect the value of the stream. A famous Hong Kong geomancer, Mr Liao (廖先生), once said that the water in nearby streams should be observed before procedures to assess the location of the site are carried out.

Shui has been classified into nine types, namely the life-giving water (养生水), water for bathing (沐浴水), water for dressing (冠带水), water for success (临官水), water for prosperity and high rank (带旺水), water for bad luck (衰水), water for the dying (病死水), water for the tomb (墓水), and water for the termination of pregnancy (绝胎水). Each type of water predicts a certain fate and divination. However, it must be noted that some names are rather misleading, for example, water for bad luck (衰水) may not necessarily mean bad fortune. On the contrary, it is supposed to bring brilliance, success, long life, comfort and all the good things in life. Some of the other names are more revealing, for example, life-giving water (养生水) brings long life and many successful grandchildren. Water for success (临官水) is believed to bring success in early life while water for the termination of pregnancy (绝胎水) is supposed to make a couple childless and estranged.

How does the geomancer computate and derive the orientation of a building or tomb? Firstly, he has to know the date of birth of the person concerned. If he is assessing a site for a building project he has to know the date and time of birth of the owner of the site. Similarly, if he is examining the site of a tomb for burial, he has to know the birth-date of the person to be buried. With the particulars of birth he refers to the *luopan* or compass to find the correct orientation (details of the compass are given in chapter 5). He then relates the year of birth to the Chinese animal year, which takes the following order: dragon (龙), snake (蛇), horse (马), goat (羊), monkey (猴), cock (难), dog (狗), pig (猪), rat (鼠), bull (牛), tiger (虎), and rabbit (兔). This order is repeated every twelve years. For example, 1880, 1892, 1904, 1916, 1928, 1940, 1952, 1964, 1976 and so on are all dragon years.

The ancient Chinese believed (some still do) that man's fate was influenced by the astrological predictions of the year of his birth. Chinese astrologers were supposed to be able to foretell the future of a newborn child by referring to those predictions. By computing the order in the cycle of the Chinese calendar, a person could be classified as belonging to one of the following orders of nature: gold (金), wood (木), water (水), fire (火), or earth (土). Since the universe too is made up of *yin-yang* and is represented by gold, wood, water, fire and earth (the Five Elements), the balance of these ingredients or elements affects nature and man's fate. To sum up, it can be said that geomancy could have originated from the divination in ancient Chinese texts some three thousand years old. By means of such divination techniques as those of the *Yi-Jing* and the theories of *yin* and *yang* and the Five Elements, the intricacy of the *feng shui* system was employed to predict and control the phenomena of nature. Had *feng shui* been developed and tested by experiment and research data it could have evolved into a branch of true science instead of remaining a form of pseudo-science.

2 The *Yin-Yang* Principles

The art of divination with regard to geomancy is closely related to the harmony of the cosmic breath—*yin* and *yang*. *The Encyclopedia Sinica* gives the following definition: "*Yin* and *yang* are the negative and positive principles of universal life". As early as the 6th century B.C. the positive and negative qualities of the *yin-yang* principles were expressed on stone drums representing the dark and bright sides of a sunlit bank.

According to the book called *Zhu Zi* (诸子), Vol. III, chapter 42, Lao Zi (老子) explained that *dao* (the way) produced oneness, which in turn produced duality (*yin* and *yang*). Then "trinity" (the *yin, yang* and harmony) resulted from the duality of the *yin* and *yang*. After that all things were evolved from trinity. The harmony of all things depends on the interaction and blending of the duality. The terms *yin* and *yang* were first used in the *Yi-Jing*. The following is quoted from the author's article "*Feng shui, Chinese Colours and Symbolism*".[1]

> "Good life is supposed to be achieved by man when he is in harmony with the flux of *yin* and *yang*. The universe too is made up of *yin-yang* and is represented by wood, fire, earth, gold and water. The balance of these ingredients or elements changes nature or man's fate. The ingredients are closely related to the seasons, directions and colours as follows:

Element	Wood	Fire	Earth	Metal	Water
Direction	East	South	Centre	West	North
Season	Spring	Summer		Autumn	Winter
Colour	Green	Red	Yellow	White	Black

1 *Journal of the Singapore Institute of Architects,* July/August, 1978.

◀ *Blessings are conveyed from the north to the south. Mountains in the north guard the site against evil forces.*

> *Yang* is bright, masculine, and powerful; *yin* is dark, feminine and totally absorbent. Both essences appear combined in various portions in all things of man, nature and the world.''

W.T. De Barry, Chan Wing Tsit and Burton Watson summarize the dual concept as follows:[2]

> "This constant reaction of the two forces on the metaphysical and physical planes was used to explain all processes of growth and change in the natural world.''

According to Joseph Needham, the philosophical use of these terms began about the beginning of the 4th century B.C. Some writers associate *yang* with heaven, vigour, the dragon and the azure colour. As far as *feng shui* is concerned, the high or raised ground and mountainous area are *yang*. *Yin* is said to represent earth, quiescence, the tiger and the orange colour. The lowlands, valley and river bank are *yin*. The Chinese called the sun *tai yang* (太阳) and the moon *tai yin* (太阴). From this the qualities of duality to the Chinese thinkers can be assessed.

²   W.T. De Barry, Chan Wing Tsit and Burton Watson, *Sources of Chinese Tradition,* London, 1960.

一
九
七
九
年
二
月
夢
霞

Landscape ▶

3 Five Elements, Ten Stems and Twelve Branches

As early as the 4th century B.C. the concept of the Five Elements or Forces was introduced by the Chinese. These elements were Wood, Fire, Earth, Metal and Water. It was also supposed to be designed in the sequence that wood gave rise to fire, fire produced earth, earth gave birth to metal, metal created water, and water made wood. In other words, wood made fire which burnt it to ashes in the form of earth which had metal in the form of ores. Metal had dew or condensation in the form of water, besides it could melt into a liquid state when heated. Water nourished plants and trees, thus producing wood.

According to the ancient Chinese the power of counteraction between the Five Elements was in accordance with the laws of nature and heaven. Thus the order of their counteraction was: water put out fire; fire melted metal; metal broke wood; wood cut into the earth; and earth absorbed water. All calamities were said to arise from disturbances of the Five Elements and the ancient Chinese were cautious not to interfere with the order of nature or cause disruptive disturbances to the natural conditions designed by heaven. The services of a geomancer were thus considered essential to determine the prevalence of the elements and forces.

The relationship of the elements with the Ten Stems and Twelve Branches, the relationship of the birth symbols with the time and the orientation and finally the chart showing the interrelationship of the Elements, the *yin-yang* principles, the Ten Stems, the Twelve Branches, the directions and the double hours of the day are shown in the following pages.

The Ten Stems and Twelve Branches

The Ten Stems, *Tian Gan*, and the Twelve Branches, *Di Zhi*, were terms introduced by the Chinese before the Hsia period (2205-1766 B.C.). For things related to the earth, they applied the names of the Branches. Each Stem or Branch was related to the *yin-yang* principles. The Ten Stems are *jia* (甲), *yi* (乙), *bing* (丙), *ding* (丁), *wu* (戊), *ji* (已), *geng* (庚), *xin* (辛), *ren* (壬), and *kui* (癸).

Jia means the sign of growth in spring and withering in winter. *Yi* indicates the triumph of life in spring or the spread of growth. *Bing* is the root of growth or blooming. *Ding* predicts the maturity of things that grow or the vegetation. *Wu* means that the growth has reached a stage of abundance and fullness. *Ji* is the order or hibernation of all things. *Geng* means the fullness leading to the need for change while *xin* indicates freshness and restoration. *Ren* is the height of function and *kui* is the preparation for spring. In other words the Ten Stems give the message of a chain reaction of nature—the growth begins in spring, reaches a stage of maturity, stops growing and renews itself. A chart of the Ten Stems is shown below:

Stem	Significance	Example	Element
JIA *YI*	Sprouting Spread of growth	tree bamboo	WOOD
BING *DING*	Blooming Maturity of things	flame light	FIRE
WU *JI*	Abundance Order of things	mountain flat land	EARTH
GENG *XIN*	Fullness Restoration	weapon utensil	METAL
REN *KUI*	Height of function Preparation for spring		WATER

The Twelve Branches are *zi* (子), *chou* (丑), *yin* (寅), *mao* (卯), *chen* (辰), *si* (巳), *wu* (午), *wei* (未), *shen* (申), *you* (酉), *shu* (戌) and *hai* (亥). *Zi* indicates the bud or the young shoot of a plant. It also signifies the beginning of all things. *Chou* literally means "tied" but actually it symbolizes the growth of things. *Yin* literally means "moved" but its significance is to lead the growing object and spread the growth. *Mao* is similar in meaning to the Stem, *wu*, as explained earlier.

Chen symbolizes progress and disregard for the old formation. *Si* means "the renewed spirit". *Wu* is the stage of maturity and *wei* signifies the smell of matured objects. *Shen* is the expanded form of maturity while *you* means ripeness. *Shu* symbolizes death and *hai* means nucleus. From this analysis the Twelve Branches are fairly similar in meaning to the Stems. Both express the chain reactions of nature.

By the combination of the Branches and Stems, the sexagenary cycle was invented and applied to the Chinese calendar as early as the 3rd century B.C. by Emperor Huang Ti's prime minister.

The Five Elements are related to the Ten Stems and Twelve Branches as follows:

Five Elements	Ten Stems	Twelve Branches
Wood (木)	*Jia* (甲) *Yi* (乙)	*Zi* (子) *Chou* (丑)
Fire (火)	*Bing* (丙) *Ding* (丁)	*Yin* (寅) *Mao* (卯)
Earth (土)	*Wu* (戊) *Ji* (己)	*Chen* (辰) *Si* (巳)
Metal (金)	*Geng* (庚) *Xin* (辛)	*Wu* (午) *Wei* (未)
Water (水)	*Ren* (壬) *Kui* (癸)	*Shen* (申) *You* (酉) *Shu* (戌) *Hai* (亥)

According to the Chinese horoscope, the configuration of the heavens at the time of the birth of a person is represented by the sign of an animal or a birth symbol. The relationship of such symbols, the orientation and the actual time or double hours are as follows:

Animal Symbol	Double Hours	Orientation
Dragon	7 a.m. - 9 a.m.	ESE
Snake	9 a.m. - 11 a.m.	SSE
Horse	11 a.m. - 1 p.m.	S
Sheep	1 p.m. - 3 p.m.	SSW
Monkey	3 p.m. - 5 p.m.	WSW
Cock	5 p.m. - 7 p.m.	W
Dog	7 p.m. - 9 p.m.	WNW
Pig	9 p.m. - 11 p.m.	NNW
Rat	11 p.m. - 1 a.m.	N
Ox	1 a.m. - 3 a.m.	NNE
Tiger	3 a.m. - 5 a.m.	ENE
Rabbit	5 a.m. - 7 a.m.	E

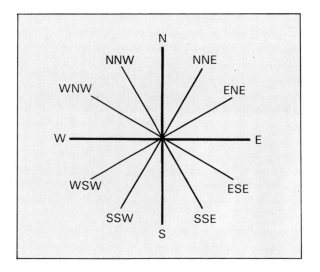

► The natural configuration of the earth's landscape exerts the beneficial influences of feng shui.

The twelve Branches are related to the animal symbols and the *yin-yang* as follows:

Branch	Symbol	*Yin-yang*
Zi	Rat	*Yin*
Chou	Ox	*Yin*
Yin	Tiger	*Yang*
Mao	Rabbit	*Yin*
Chen	Dragon	*Yang*
Si	Snake	*Yang*
Wu	Horse	*Yang*
Wei	Sheep	*Yang*
Shen	Monkey	*Yin*
You	Cock	*Yang*
Shu	Dog	*Yin*
Hai	Pig	*Yin*

A final chart derived from the above three charts summarizes this section.

Five Elements	*Yin-yang*	Ten Stems	Twelve Branches	Orientation	Double hours
Wood	*Yin*	*Jia*	*Zi*	N	11 p.m. - 1 a.m.
	Yin	*Yi*	*Chou*	NNE	1 a.m. - 3 a.m.
Fire	*Yang*	*Bing*	*Yin*	ENE	3 a.m. - 5 a.m.
	Yin	*Ding*	*Mao*	E	5 a.m. - 7 a.m.
Earth	*Yang*	*Wu*	*Chen*	ESE	7 a.m. - 9 a.m.
	Yang	*Ji*	*Si*	SSE	9 a.m. - 11 a.m.
Metal	*Yang*	*Geng*	*Wu*	S	11 a.m. - 1 p.m.
	Yang	*Xin*	*Wei*	SSW	1 p.m. - 3 p.m.
Water	*Yin*	*Ren*	*Shen*	WSW	3 p.m. - 5 p.m.
	Yang	*Kui*	*You*	W	5 p.m. - 7 p.m.
	Yin		*Shu*	WNW	7 p.m. - 9 p.m.
	Yin		*Hai*	NNW	9 p.m. - 11 p.m.

4 Trigrams or Hexagrams

In order to comprehend the geomancer's compass or *luopan* we have to know the meaning of the Eight Trigrams which occupy the first circle of the *luopan*. The symbol of the Eight Trigrams had two forms; the original form was attributed to Fu-Hsi, the first legendary ruler (2852 B.C.) in the 12th century B.C. It was changed and amended by King Wen. The *Yi-Jing* (易经) (one of the Five Canonical Classics) was based on the symbol of the Eight Trigrams.

The Eight Trigrams (八卦) indicate the eight points of the compass represented by a primitive numerical system. They are invested with the qualities and symbolic meanings according to the way in which *yin* and *yang* lines are combined and they apply to all possible relations of life. A drawing of it is shown below.

The Eight Trigrams

Below are Trigrams illustrated in the *Imperial Encyclopedia* of the 18th century A.D. A was devised during the Sui dynasty (581-618 A.D.) while the rest are Tang (618-907 A.D.).

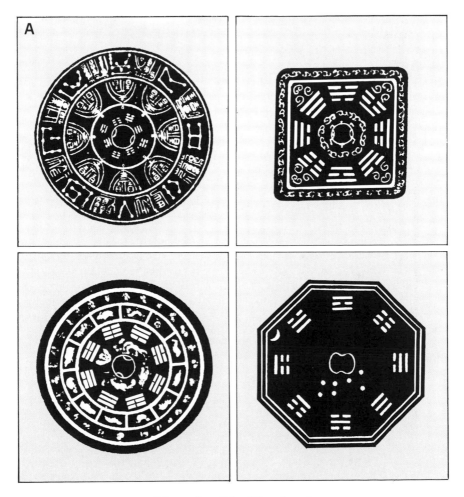

Trigrams from Sui and Tang dynasties

The relationship of the Eight Trigrams and *feng shui* divination can be summed up thus: When the Great Extreme or *Tai Ji* (太极) was formed it produced the two complementary powers of *yin* and *yang* which gave birth to the four primary symbols. The Eight Trigrams, originating from these symbols, determine the divination of fortune. The orientation of buildings or tombstones is determined by the geomancer as he reads from the compass which has the direction or orientation represented by the Eight Trigrams as follows:

☰	乾	*qian*	North-west
	坤	*kun*	South-west
	辰	*zhen*	East
	坎	*kan*	North
	艮	*ken*	North-east
	巽	*sun*	South-east
	离	*li*	South
	兑	*dui*	West

The symbols or lines of the Trigrams' numerical system were derived by sages as early as 2860 B.C. to give indications of their expressions in fortune-telling. There are two kinds of lines: a broken line and a solid line. The broken line -- indicates *yin* and the solid line — *yang*. Each solid line in turn symbolizes the dragon which has always been recognized by the Chinese as a symbol of vigilance, strength, the virtues of Heaven and the minister of the will of the gods.

The word *qian* symbolizes heaven, creativity and originality of all things. Of the Eight Trigrams it is the one to indicate change, variation or substitution of things to achieve harmony. As indicated by the strong and undivided lines of the Trigrams (☰), it means good fortune, strength and vitality.

Kun means "reception". It represents the earth and femininity. Expressing originality and firmness, it is complementary to *qian* and it contains all things which through its power achieve full development. Numerically it is represented by three broken lines (☷) which symbolize an accentuation of the *yin* qualities and subordination.

Zhen pertaining to geomancy means "thunder". For the interpretation of the Eight Trigrams it symbolizes the movement and development of things. Indicated by two broken lines and one solid line (☳), it foretells apprehension and changes.

Kan literally means "pit". It also expresses danger. Another meaning is "water flowing" which signifies the thinking and concentration of the mind. The solid line in the centre (☵) symbolizes the strength of inner thought; it also spells the perilous danger that might be encountered or the mental abnormality that might be suffered.

Ken means "mountain". In geomancy it signifies that action or motion is prevented or halted. In the numerical system it is represented by a solid line with two broken lines below (☶). Since it represents a mountain it symbolizes the stoppage of travellers and signifies the concept of resting of both mind and body.

Sun means penetration and denotes the sun as well as the wind and wood. Thus it reflects the qualities of pliability and influence. It is represented by two solid lines and a broken line (☴). Sometimes it is used to signify the growth of vegetation.

The word *li* means separation. But in fortune-telling and geomancy it denotes firmness and beauty and it bears the sign of fire. Represented by a solid line at the top and the bottom with a broken line in between (☲), it has a double meaning of inhering in and adhering to.

Dui is a joy, happiness and satisfaction. It signifies achievement and progression. Represented by a broken line and two solid lines (☱), its weakness is compensated by the double portion of power and strength.

The following chart shows how the Eight Trigrams are related to the Five Elements and how they are associated with the animals and the seasons.

Trigram	Element	Associated Animal	Emblem	Associated Season	Associated Time of Day	Interpretation
qian	Metal	dragon, horse	heaven	late autumn	early night	strength, roundness & vitality
kun	Earth	mare, ox	earth	late summer, early autumn	afternoon	nourishment or squareness
zhen	Wood	galloping horse or flying dragon	thunder	spring	morning	movement, roads or bamboo sprouts
kan	Water	pig	moon and water	mid-winter	midnight	curved things, wheels, mental abnormality, danger
ken	Wood	dog, rat and birds	mountain	early spring	early morning	gates, fruits, seeds
sun	Wood	hen	wind	late spring, early summer	morning	growth, vegetative force
li	Fire	pheasant, toad, crab, snail, tortoise	lightning	summer	midday	weapons, drought and brightness
dui	Water and Metal	sheep	sea-water	mid-autumn	evening	reflections and mirror images

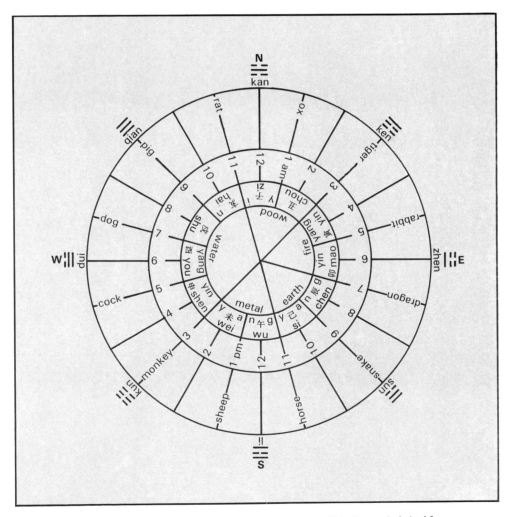

Diagram illustrating the interpretation of the Eight Trigrams. This diagram is derived from the charts worked out in the previous pages. It shows the relationship of the Eight Trigrams with the animal symbols, the Five Elements and the time of day.

5 Methods for the Divination of *Feng Shui*

There are various methods for the divination of *feng shui*. One method is called the Ancestral Hall or Direction method which emphasizes the relationship of the planets with the Eight Trigrams. There is a *yin* and *yang* for all things. If harmony is not achieved they destroy each other. For example, if a thing or a part of nature is of *yin,* it must face the *yin* direction (refer to the chart on the Five Elements and their relationship with other factors of influence on page 20). According to Wang Wei this method was practised in Zhejiang, China.

Another type is called the Jiangxi method as its practice originated south of the Yangzi River in China. This method is quite commonly practised in the Southeast Asian region. Its theory is based on the understanding of the landscape—the profiles of the land, the sources of rivers, the terrain, etc. Just like the geomancy specialist for tomb layout, the Jiangxi practitioner believes in the five factors, namely, *loong, xue, sha, shui* and *xiang.*

The advance or retreat of the dragon, i.e. the ups and downs of the profile of the land, is of vital importance to the quality of the site. The ground must be hard and solid and must have a good profile like that of the real dragon if it is to be rated as a good site. The sand on the ground and the water sources are also of great importance to the Jiangxi geomancer. Diagrams showing the relationship of sites to the water courses are given on pages 70 to 73.

For both the Direction method and the Jiangxi method the *luopan* or geomancer's compass is employed to determine the orientation of buildings. Perhaps the easiest method for a Chinese scholar is to learn to read the *tong shu* (通书) or Chinese calendar as it contains one or two pages of text and diagrams rendering some brief guides regarding the burial time and orientations of tombstones.

◀ *Mountain ranges of impressive height exert the* yang *energy while low hilly sites express the* yin *force.*

Luopan *or Geomancer's Compass*

The *luopan* is the geomancer's instrument for the divination of orientations of buildings or tombstones. There are several types of *luopan*, some more complicated than others. They serve to represent the universe by means of which forces of heaven and earth can be harmonized. The manual explaining the usage of the *luopan* depends on its designer and its manufacturer. It is not within the scope of this book to explain each operational method or the art of divination by the use of each type of *luopan*. Moreover, the application of *feng shui* is not specific. Very often two professors of geomancy give different interpretations of the *feng shui* of a particular site or building at the same time.

A simple *luopan* has as few as five concentric circles of Chinese characters while a complicated one has as many as thirty-four. Most of them are discs of lacquered wood. The latest model has a metal casing or finish. The disc is set into a square base often made of lacquered wood; the cheaper ones have a plastic base. The background of the disc is usually black and the Chinese characters are in gold or red. It carries a mariner's compass with a floating needle in the centre under a piece of glass. A drawing of the simplest net tablet or *luopan* with five concentric rings is shown on the next page.

Another simple *luopan* is shown on page 33. This has seven concentric tiers. The first is divided into twenty-four positions showing the names of the heavenly stars for the divination of the qualities of the dragon at the site. The second tier also has twenty-four places. It is derived from the *bagua,* the Stems and the Branches. It is used for the assessment of orientation. The third tier contains the numerals from one to nine. The sum of two opposite numerals always makes ten. The fourth tier is subdivided into as many as sixty-four positions which are used for the divination of the sand or *sha* of the site. The fifth and sixth tiers are compositions of the *bagua,* the Stems and the Branches, while the seventh shows the position of the dragon by the compositions of the Stems and the Branches.

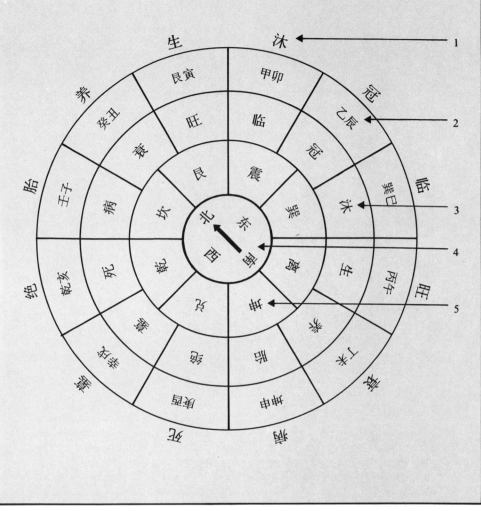

Luopan A

1 Indicates the twelve main types of "water".

2 Indicates the five orders of nature, *yin-yang* and the time of birth.

3 The types of "water".

4 The four cardinal points.

5 hexagram (八卦) derived from *Yi-Jing*. Each word represents a direction, e.g. 乾 : North-west.

More complicated *luopans* usually show the Eight Trigrams in the arrangement of *Fu-Hsi* denoting the eight directions of the compass. Another type of *luopan* contains the *bagua* in the first ring and the Stems and Branches in the next few rings. The second circle consists of the time or hour of day classified under *chou* (丑), *yin* (寅), *wu* (午), *you* (酉), *wei* (未), *shen* (申), *chen* (辰), and *si* (巳), and four of the Ten Stems, *kui* (癸), *xin* (辛), *ding* (丁), and *bing* (丙). This *luopan* has thirty-six concentric circles. The twenty-four divisions of the compass are shown on the sixth circle. The seventh tier represents the Ten Stems. The eighth repeats the five orders of nature twelve times. The eleventh tier is divided into three hundred and sixty equal blanks representing the degrees of a circle. This is repeated at the sixteenth and the twentieth strata. Here the blanks are painted gold and red at every fifth place to indicate the good or desirable positions. The twelfth stratum shows the Ten Stems repeated six times. The numerals from one to nine are repeated on the twenty-third, twenty-fourth, thirty-first and thirty-fourth tiers in the arrangement of the magic square. The most important thing to note of this *luopan* is the thirty-fifth circle which is divided into three hundred and sixty parts. Some parts are golden with red dots, while others are blank or bear the sign of an arrow or figures. The golden parts with red dots are the positions bearing good omens.

The *luopan* shown on page 35 is an antique (over a hundred years old). It is made of a yellow lacquered wood disc on a red lacquered square base. The red threads are fixed, dividing the disc into four equal areas. The mariner's compass is placed below the glass disc. This *luopan* has twenty-four concentric rings. The first is occupied by the Eight Trigrams in occult signs. The second to the fourth contain the five orders of nature, the Stems and Branches as well as the *bagua* in occult terms. The fifth circle represents the twenty-four divisions of the compass, while the sixth is divided into seventy-two parts each containing two characters of the sexagenary circle, written one above the other and arranged in groups of five divided by blank spaces. The Stems, Branches and Trigrams are used again in the outer circles and repeated with the exception of the eighteenth, twenty-second, twenty-third and twenty-fourth rows. The eighteenth row consists of numerals only. Again the most important circle is the second last tier. Just like the previous *luopan* the circle is divided into three hundred and sixty parts of either black crosses or gold and red dots. Black crosses denote bad luck while red dots signify good fortune.

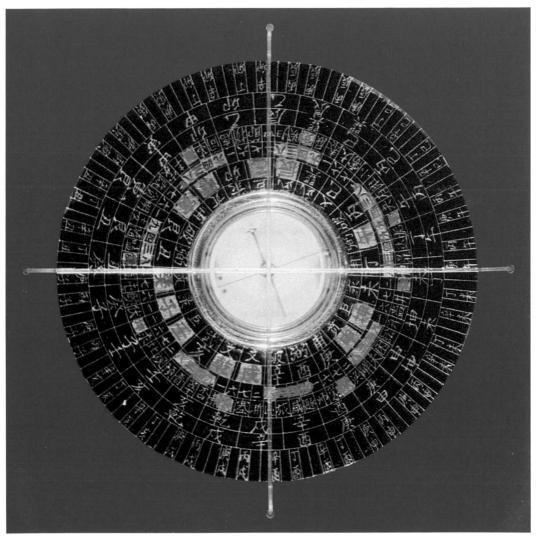

Luopan B

Luopan C

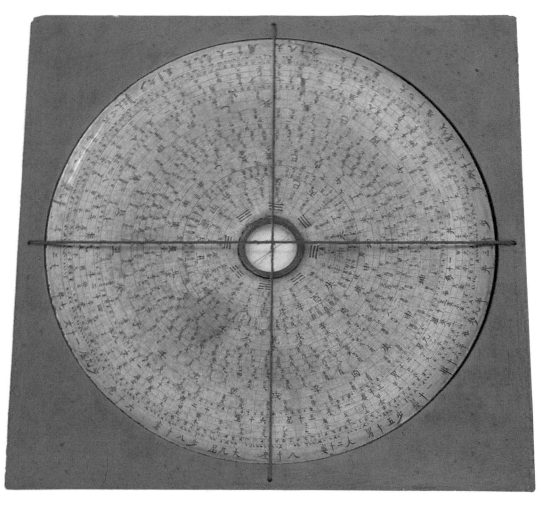

Luopan D

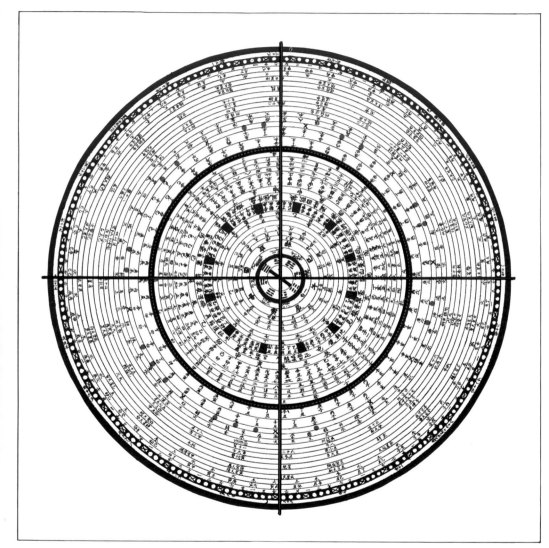

Luopan E

The *luopan* E is commonly sold in Taiwan. As usual, the first two circles show the Eight Trigrams in correct sequence. The third concentric circle known as the *ba sha huang quan* (八煞黄泉) is used to gauge the position of the dragon at the site. The fourth, called *ba lu huang quan* (八路黄泉), is employed to find the quality of the water courses. The fifth is the circle of the ''stars'' to ascertain the good or bad qualities of the dragon. The next ring indicates the positions of the mariner's needle. It gives the direction for the burial of the dead according to *yin-yang* principles. The seventh circle is blank but the eighth is divided into twenty-four parts related to the Five Elements. The ninth contains the Stems and the Branches to predict good or bad luck. The tenth shows the seventy-two positions of the dragon while the eleventh is derived from the oracle system of Chou Yi (周易) during the period of the Three Kingdoms (220-581 A.D.). Following it the twelfth ring is divided into twenty-four positions which are derived from the *bagua,* the Stems and the Branches. These positions also indicate the twenty-four stars for divination.

The thirteenth circle looks complicated as it is subdivided into sixty places with words which are composed of two characters, each taken in serial order from the Branches. It is used mainly for the divination of burial grounds. The fourteenth tier, called *tou di qi men* (透地奇門) spells sixty numbers or positions of good or bad luck. The fifteenth tier is derived from the oracle bones called *tou di lian shan* (透地连山). The sixteenth has sixty positions and is related to the fifteenth tier and the twenty-eight ''star'' positions to determine the sand of the site. The seventeenth tier also has sixty divining positions for the prediction of fortune. For the divination of natural phenomena the eighteenth tier gives twenty-four places which are related to the *bagua,* the Stems and the Branches. The nineteenth tier is divided into two hundred and forty parts for the divination of burial grounds. Following it is a ring of forty-eight positions which are compositions of the Stems and Branches. The twenty-first circle is also for the divination of tombstone positions. It is quite similar in function to the twentieth and twenty-first circles. The twenty-second predicts the positions of *sha qi* (煞气) or evil influence shown by the sign of a cross (✕). The circles (●) coloured red indicate positions of separation and emptiness. The circles coloured yellow are directions of good fortune and luck. The following tier is again divided into sixty positions, each occupied by a word which conveys fate and divination.

The twenty-fourth tier is related solely to the Five Elements while the twenty-fifth is derived from the words representing the twelve heavenly planets which are devised for assessment of geomantic sand. The twenty-sixth speaks of the relationship of the "stars" with the orientation of the cities. For a "correct" burial time, the twenty-seventh tier is used. The positions on this tier are related to the angles of the sun in the sky. The twenty-eighth circle is related to the twenty-seventh and it is derived from the names of heavenly guards or warriors. The next tier indicates the twelve heavenly *xian* (仙) or gods for the prediction of an auspicious time for burial, moving into a new house or erecting the main post or ridge beam of a house or temple. For the offering of prayers or for the burial of the dead the thirteenth tier is used. The next tier spells the names of the twenty-four heavenly stars and it is for geomantic burial purposes. The Five Elements again are used in the thirty-second tier for the choice of a site. The next ring consists of the sixty combinations of the Ten Stems and the Twelve Branches. It is used for finding the dragon or the *xue* of the site. Repetitions of the numerals 1, 3, 5, 7, 9, appear in the thirty-fourth ring. The figures on the opposite sides are always similar. The thirty-fifth is the most important ring as it gives divination of good or ill fortune or good or bad site. The dots coloured red indicate good signs while the crosses spell a bad omen. The last ring bears the names of the twenty-eight heavenly stars and is used for the divination of the environment.

How to Read the Luopan

The *luopan* is placed with its base parallel to the door or wall of the building or object to be orientated according to *feng shui*. The disc is rotated until the mariner's compass coincides with or overlaps the red marking of the central disc under the glass piece. The red strings or plastic threads that divide the disc into four areas give the reading of the four orientations of the object or building. Different *luopans* differ in detail and it is beyond the scope of this book to discuss how they vary. However, it can be explained simply that if the string overlaps the second last circle of the disc at the spots that spell good omen the orientation is considered desirable; otherwise it is to be avoided.

The Geomancer's Ruler

The orientation of a building and its doors are not the only factors considered important in the divination of *feng shui*. The size of the rooms and the overall dimensions of a building are also carefully checked in order to ensure the endorsement of good fortune and posterity.

The drawing on the next page shows the geomancer's ruler specially made to measure (43 cm x 5 cm) and reduced to a scale of 1:4. It is used to check the dimensions of a building. It is divided into eight parts and each part is subdivided into four sections. The first part (reading from right to left) is *cai* (財) or prosperity while the last is *ben* (本) or origin. Both are considered fortunate markings. The dimensions reckoned to bring fortune and wealth are multiples of 43 cm. The second part is *bing* (病) or illness. Any dimension that falls into this section spells a bad omen such as losing a marriage partner, or fortune or job. The third part is *li* (离) or separation. Again this conveys the presage of bad luck and separation. The fourth is *ee* (義) or righteousness and it predicts prosperity, posterity and security. The fifth, *guan* (官) or official, is a sign of good fortune, eminence and promotion. The sixth, *jie* (劫) or robbed, gives an extremely unfortunate prediction as it spells death, misfortune and separation. The seventh, *hai* (害) or harm foretells calamity, death, illness and quarrel. Summing up, a chart of measurements (good or bad) can be simplified as follows:

BAD DIMENSIONS

(1) $5\frac{3}{8}$ to $16\frac{1}{8}$ cm

(2) $26\frac{7}{8}$ to $37\frac{5}{8}$ cm

(3) Multiples of 43 added to (1) or (2), e.g. 4306, 4330 cm

GOOD DIMENSIONS

(a) 0 to $5\frac{3}{8}$ cm

(b) $16\frac{1}{8}$ to $26\frac{7}{8}$ cm

(c) $37\frac{5}{8}$ to $48\frac{3}{8}$ cm

(d) Multiples of 43 cm, e.g. 4300 cm, 4343 cm

(e) Multiples of 43 added to either (a), (b) or (c)

本				害				刦				官				義				離				病				財			
興旺	進室	篁斜	財至	口古	病臨	死諡	災至	財夹	離鄉	退口	死刵	官置	進益	橫財	順斜	天吉	書子	益財	添丁	失脫	官鬼	刦財	長庚	孤寡	牢执	公事	退財	逆招	六合	金庫	財德

Geomancer's Ruler

Wooden Geomancer's Ruler

Feng Shui *Messages in the Chinese Calendar*

A simple and easy way of practising *feng shui* divination without consulting a geomancer or having the necessary knowledge or equipment is to read the Chinese calendar or *tong shu* (通书).

Historical Background of the Chinese Calendar

Legend has it that Huang Di (黄帝) (2697 B.C.) was the first to order his astronomers to study the stars and prepare a calendar. His minister Da Yao (大尧) invented a system called *chia zi* (甲子).[1] Three hundred and forty years later, during the Yao (尧) period, the *xia* (夏) calendar was made by Xi (義) and He (和) who calculated the signs, the sun, the moon and the constellations.[2] During the Shang period (商纪) (1766-1154 B.C.) a sixty-day calendar was used. Each day was designed by a combination of two characters, each taken in serial order from the *Tian Gan* or the Ten Heavenly Stems and the *Di Zhi* or Twelve Earthly Branches respectively.[3] The sixty-day cycle was then applied to the year. To achieve this the sixty-day cycle was divided into six ten-day units called *xun* (旬) and one to three ten-day units were interrelated.[4] From the Chou dynasty (周纪) (1122-255 B.C.) the *Tian Gan* was correlated with the Five Elements and also with the *yin* and *yang*. *Di Zhi* was applied to the solar months. Animal symbols were created in the 6th century B.C. to correspond to the twelve characters of the *Di Zhi*.[5]

To chart the seasons, the twelve months of the solar year were divided into twenty-four half-months, twelve of which were called *zhong qi* (中气) and the remaining twelve *jie qi* (节气).

---

[1]   Si Ma Qian (司马千) and Yi Feng (涵芬) (*See Chi,* or *The Records,* 1916.)
[2]   W.E. Soothill, *The Hall of Light,* Lutterworth Press, London, 1951, p. 57.
[3]   C.S. Wong, *A Cycle of Chinese Festivities,* Singapore, 1967, p. 10. Please refer to table on p. 20.
[4]   Joseph Needham, op. cit., Vol. III, p. 397.
[5]   Ibid., pp. 322, 389 and 397.

Leo Wieger gave an account of the adjustments made to the Chinese calendar of 104 B.C.[6] It was Liu Hong (刘洪) who observed that the solstitial points were not fixed and that the equator and the ecliptic were not one and the same thing. Liu Hong's calendar which was adopted during the period of the Three Kingdoms (三国) was modified by Jing Xi (经西) in 385 A.D. The accuracy of the calendar was maintained throughout the Sui (随纪) (581-617 A.D.) and the Tang dynasties (唐纪) (618-906 A.D.) The new calendars were made during the Sung dynasty (宋纪) (960-1278 A.D.) and C.S. Wong related that two more were prepared during the Ming dynasty (明纪) (1368-1628 A.D.). One was called the *da tong li* (大统历) while the other, the *hui hui li* (回回历) prepared by Zhu Dai Yu (朱戴育), proved to be rather inaccurate.

A Jesuit revised calendar was used as the Imperial Calendar from the reign of Kang Xi (康熙) (1662-1723 A.D.) until 1912 when it was abolished by the government. However, this lunisolar calendar continued to be used by the people who called it the farmer's calendar or *nong li* (农历). Some Singaporean Chinese still use it and they too call it the *nong li*. Usually it is printed and compiled in Hong Kong in the form of an annotated annual almanac called the *tong shu*, sold for S$4 per copy.[7]

The *Feng Shui* Predictions

Usually a drawing of the Eight Trigrams with the stars, the Stems, the Branches and predictions is shown on the first or second page of the *tong shu*. Rules-of-thumb on the orientations of tombstones and dates for burial are given according to the year. One year always differs from another and the predictions change every year. A photograph of the drawing is shown on the next page.

---

6   Leo Wieger, *China Throughout the Ages,* China, 1928, p. 106.
7   There are 365.25 days in the calendar year, whereas a lunar month averages only 29.5306 days, thus giving only 354 actual days in the entire year. According to the *tong shu* an intercalated month in every three years (tropical) and two intercalated months in every five years are added. This intercalated month is called a *run yue* (润月).

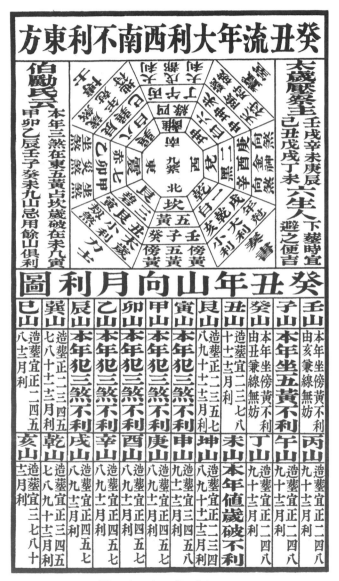

The orientation of tombstones as explained in the tong shu.

6 Standard Rules-of-Thumb of Geomancy

According to the geomancer accurate and detailed predictions can be given only after careful study, analysis and observation of the site. The orientation of a building and the planning of a house can be computed by the use of a *luopan* with reference to the birth date and time of birth of the owner. As it is rather expensive to engage the services of a geomancer perhaps knowing the standard rules-of-thumb of *feng shui* may be of use and interest.

Some practices of geomancy originated out of practical reasons which can be listed as follows:

(a) Geomancers always recommend that buildings should be constructed on high ground instead of in a valley. Surely this is a practical suggestion as low-lying areas may be easily flooded.

(b) In all books on geomancy it is written that the occupants of a house standing on the triangular lot at a "Y" junction will suffer from fire outbreaks and other calamities. This sounds rather severe and unreasonable but on closer examination it can be seen that vehicles are accident-prone at "Y" junctions. Moreover a triangular lot is difficult to handle in terms of landscaping and planning.

(c) Many geomancers believe that trees on the northwest side of the site protect the house and bring happiness to the family, but very few are able to explain the logic or the origin. When an analysis of the geographical features of China is made it can be seen that the northwesterly winds bring along yellow dust from the Mongolian border. Big trees planted on the northwest side thus protect the dwelling from the polluted wind.

(d) Trees are not always "protective" towards the household. Sometimes they obstruct the "entry of wealth". For example, a big tree planted in front of the main door deprives the tenants of fortune. This idea could have originated from the fact that a big tree being shady deprives the house and the occupants from much welcomed sunshine. Another practical reason could be that such big trees are usually tall and thus good conductors of lightning.

(e) If a building is located at the end of a narrow street it will be an "unfortunate" dwelling. This sounds illogical or superstitious. Perhaps from past experience it was found that in times of danger or during an outbreak of fire, the fire brigade found it difficult to reach the building. Even the tenants might have difficulty getting out of the narrow lane to get help.

(f) However, it does not mean that buildings situated on the main road are sure to bring good luck and health. A desirable position could only be obtained if the main road was to the west of the building. Architecturally, in tropical countries, it is practical to have a building located on the eastern side of the road because in so doing the western wall/walls can be built solid to give privacy and to act as a noise buffer as well as to avoid the sun when it is in the west. But in temperate countries the sun is always welcome.

(g) In China the south-westerly winds during summer are most refreshing. The geomancer's insistence on having a vacant lot to the south for good fortune can be looked upon as practical by the architects of the tropical region because the southern side is ideal for an open field or garden. Windows and doors facing the north and south sides do not get the full impact of the hot sun as shown in the sketch (Plan A). To people living in the temperate zones vacant land in any direction is always an amenity.

(h) The geomancer always recommends that the most important area of a building should be located centrally. For example, in a house the living room which is indeed the "hub" and focal point should be at the centre. This is practical as it reduces circulation space and saves time when occupants walk from their rooms to the living area. For tropical countries Plan A is suitable.

(i) Harm will befall young people should their bedrooms be located next to the kitchen. This sounds superstitious but on closer examination it is a practical point to consider. Should the kitchen be next to the bedrooms the latter would be badly polluted. Moreover fires often start from the kitchen in domestic buildings.

(j) A house or a building must have a back door which is not in line with the front door as shown in Plan A. If the back and front doors are in line as in Plan B, fortune cannot be retained. A house without a back door spells death and misfortune. This appears irrational but without a back exit it certainly causes inconvenience to the housewife as she often has to go to the backyard where the rubbish bins and clothes-lines are placed.

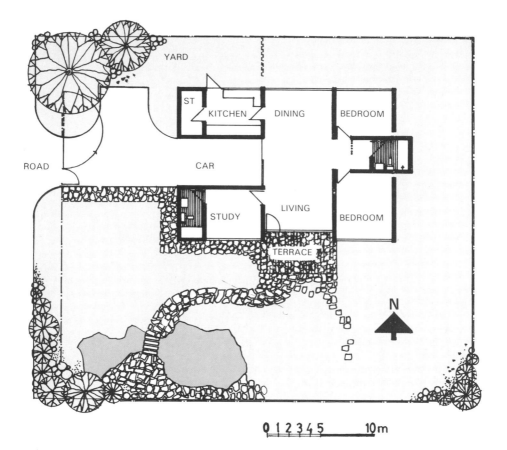

PLAN A

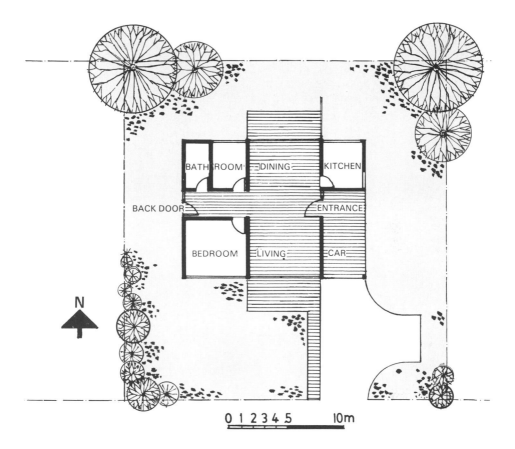

0 1 2 3 4 5   10m

PLAN B

Other geomantic rules which originated out of practical reasons are shown in Chinese brush sketches below and in the following pages.

1

2

1   *The site with the White Tiger and the Azure Dragon*
    The ideal feng shui *is shown in this painting by the author. The houses are sited on a "horseshoe" fertile site bounded by the "Azure Dragon" of the* yang *mountainous range on the left, the "White Tiger" of the* yin *hilly site on the right and the lofty mountain at the back (north). On the south a calm meandering stream flows by. It is believed that blessings are transmitted from the north to the south as good cosmic breath comes down the slope this way. The mountain in the north protects the site from evil influences.*

2   *House on the side of a mountain*
    The geomancer feels that to be sited near steeply falling water on the side of a mountain is highly dangerous.

3   *House near a graveyard*
    It is unfortunate to have the dwelling orientated south of a graveyard as it would be disturbed by evil forces.

3

4

5

4 *House with evil influences*
Trees planted near the front gate spell evil influences.

5 *House between two roads*
If a dwelling is located in between two roads frequent thefts may befall the family.

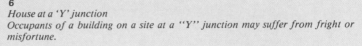

6
House at a 'Y' junction
Occupants of a building on a site at a "Y" junction may suffer from fright or misfortune.

6

7 *House on a site signifying separation*
The painting shows a situation whereby the "dragon" and the "tiger" flow towards one another in the form of water signifying the separation of family members.

8 *House near a pool at the West*
A pool or pond at the western side of the house is a bad omen as the west is symbolized by the White Tiger. A pool situated in this direction means that the White Tiger is opening its mouth and it may devour "wealth" or human life.

7   8

9

9 *Water courses should be seen and harsh-looking rocky formation should be camouflaged by* feng shui *trees*

Comic sketch

10 A: *"Why was the construction of this house abandoned?"*

B: *"The owner has spent a great deal of money in building the artificial hill at the back and the rubble wall in front and to the northeast to ward off evil influences and bring luck. He has exhausted his building funds. I guess his luck will come when he has saved enough to proceed with the construction!"*

11 *House with ill luck*
Ill luck is supposed to befall a family if a stream flows across the site of its house. It is believed that the stream will "carry off" the wealth of the family and the good personal qualities of the descendants. This could have been the result of calamities and other problems due to frequent flooding.

12 *House with a tree with evil forces*
Fast-growing trees should not be planted in the courtyard as they may be attacked by evil forces.

12

Admittedly not all practices in geomancy are of practical origin. Some emerged from ancient theories of mysticism while others emerged from superstition, for example, (a) to (g) on pages 59 and 60.

▼ *Door gods of the Wak Hai Cheng Bio Temple, Singapore.*

Door gods of Hong San Temple, Singapore.

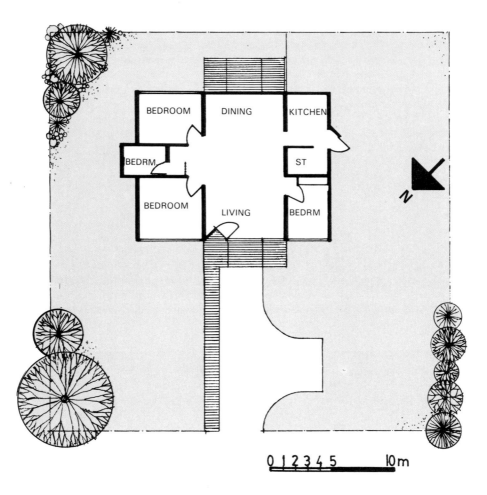

PLAN C

External doors and bedroom doors are fixed at an oblique angle to avoid the direction of the door of the devil.

(a)   An old legend reveals that in ancient times there grew on Mount Du Su (度朔山) in the northeastern sea a huge blossom tree which covered an area of a few thousand square miles. The lowest branches inclined towards the northeast and all those who went near were devoured by demons. The evil spirits were later conquered by the good spirits called Shen Shu (神荼) and Yu Lei (鬱垒). Since then people have painted the portraits of these good spirits on their main doors to ward off evil influences, hence they are also called door gods. It has since become essential for temple buildings to have the door gods painted on the front doors.

This superstitious belief spread as far as Japan and temples and pagodas were constructed at the northeastern part of the Imperial Palace in Japan to block the evil spirits. Therefore the northeast is said to be "the door of the devil" (鬼门) and the southwest the "back door of the devil" (后鬼门). Should doors be made along these directions bad luck and ill health would befall the occupants. If a building is orientated along the "door of the devil" its doors must be relocated or designed at an oblique angle to avoid calamity and evil spirits as shown in Plan C.

(b)   Contrary to belief surrounding the northeast, the south is reputed to be of good orientation. There is an old saying in Chinese: *chao nan er chen wang* (朝南而成王). It means that if one is orientated towards the south one would become a king. This appears to be utterly optimistic, but in the tropical regions orientating one's dwelling towards the south is certainly a wise idea as it does not get the full impact when the sun is in the west.

(c)   Good *chi* (气) or cosmic breath comes down a slope from north to south. Not only should the south be vacant to benefit from the *yang,* the other three sides must be closed to "accumulate" the good influences. A hill on the northern side is ideal as it protects the site from malignant implications. It is even better when the south slopes down to a river or a sea. Many temples in Singapore were planned in such a manner during the early nineteenth century. Guan Yin Tong in Singapore is a vivid example. (See the photograph on page 76.)

(d) The reverse situation, i.e. to have the front portion higher than the rear, means that the occupants would be cut off from their relatives or family.

(e) Even the number of bedrooms a building contains affects the *feng shui*. A building or house having one, two, five, six, seven or nine bedrooms is considered good but one with three, four or eight bedrooms symbolizes ill-fortune.

(f) The theory of the Five Elements is applied to the practice of geomancy. Very often the *feng shui* diviner insists that the kitchen should face either east or south as he believes that the orders of nature must not be upset. Wood is related to the east while fire is related to the south. Therefore, to orientate the kitchen towards a direction related to wood or fire is surely a good practice.

(g) Similarly it is necessary to apply the theory of *yin* and *yang* when placing the well or source of water supply. According to geomancers the water in the well is *yin* and the fire of the stove is *yang*. *Yin* and *yang* are of opposite principles. To place a stove next to a well is unwise as calamity might befall the tenants.

There is an interesting example of *feng shui* practice resulting from old habits. It appears that during ancient times in China the amount of taxes on houses was collected and gauged by the width or frontage of the building. The residents succeeded in paying less tax by making their houses as narrow as they possibly could. Since then it was thought that a narrow frontage brought "luck" to the residents. Architectural satisfaction of such a design for a house seems difficult to achieve.

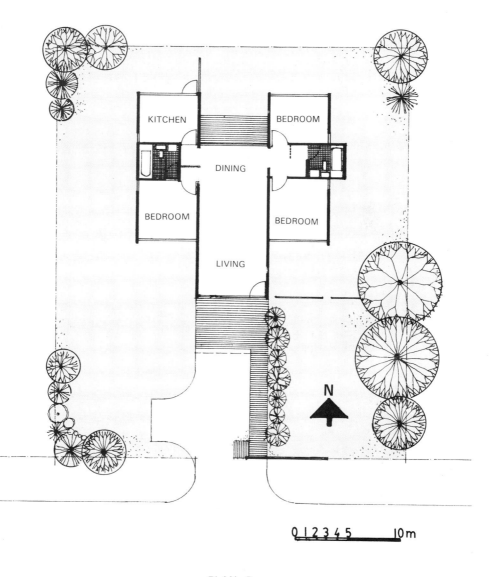

KITCHEN

BEDROOM

DINING

BEDROOM

BEDROOM

LIVING

N

0 1 2 3 4 5   10 m

PLAN   D

*A house with narrow frontage. Architecturally it is difficult to treat the
roof form of the living room.*

The following chart shows the roof plan of buildings or houses and how *feng shui* affects the occupants. It is based on the data and information obtained from the *Imperial Encyclopedia* (written in classical Chinese) and other sources.

 Shape of building	Omen	Effect of *feng shui* on the occupants
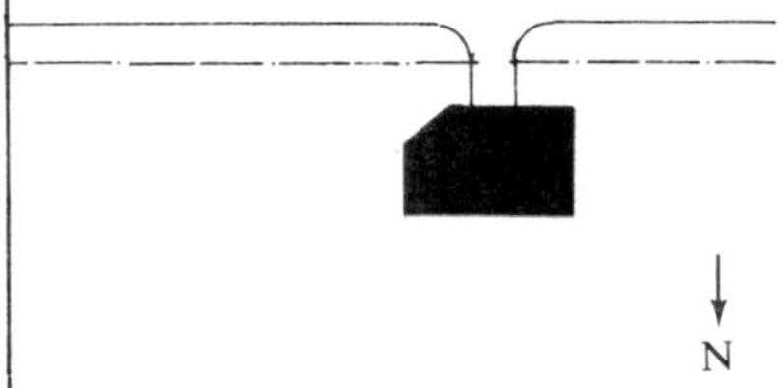	Good	Wealth will be accrued but the occupants will not have the blessing of descendants.
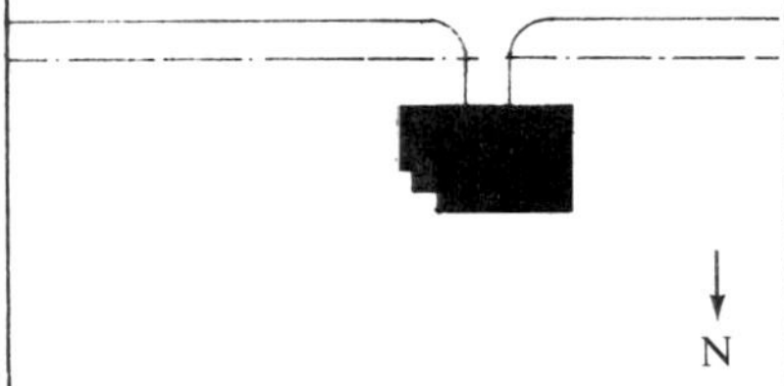	Good	Wealth will be accumulated and riches will be enjoyed.
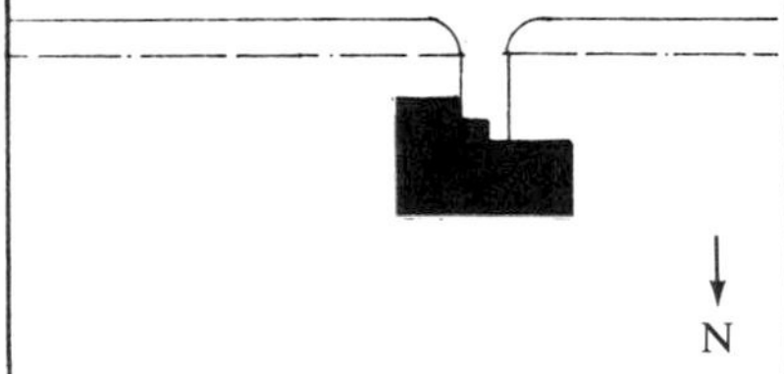	Bad	Descendants will be unintelligent and wealth will not be enjoyed.
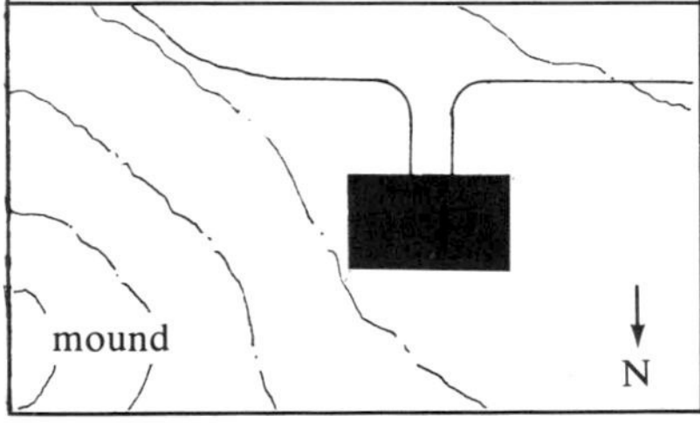	Bad	Descendants will not survive. Death will occur in the family.

Shape of building	Omen	Effect of *feng shui* on the occupants
stream ... N	**Bad**	Even though riches could be obtained at an early stage of life, poverty would be suffered at the later stage.
mound ... N	**Good**	Descendants will be fortunate even though they meet with failure at the earlier stage of life.
N	**Good**	Sons will be officials of the government and daughters will be married to well-established officials.
N ... hill	**Good**	Members of the family will be strong and healthy and well established.

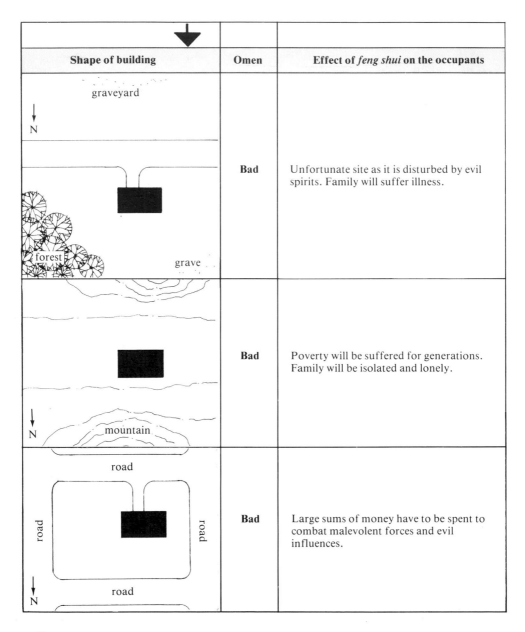

Shape of building	Omen	Effect of *feng shui* on the occupants
graveyard ↓ N forest grave	**Bad**	Unfortunate site as it is disturbed by evil spirits. Family will suffer illness.
↓ N mountain	**Bad**	Poverty will be suffered for generations. Family will be isolated and lonely.
road road road ↓ N road	**Bad**	Large sums of money have to be spent to combat malevolent forces and evil influences.

Shape of building	Omen	Effect of *feng shui* on the occupants
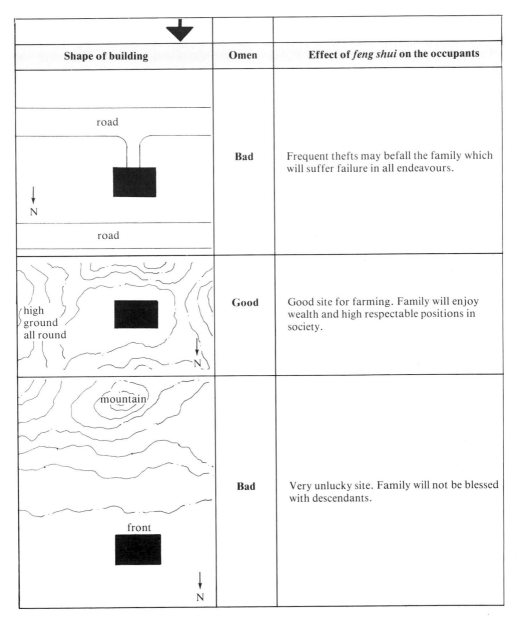	**Bad**	Frequent thefts may befall the family which will suffer failure in all endeavours.
	Good	Good site for farming. Family will enjoy wealth and high respectable positions in society.
	Bad	Very unlucky site. Family will not be blessed with descendants.

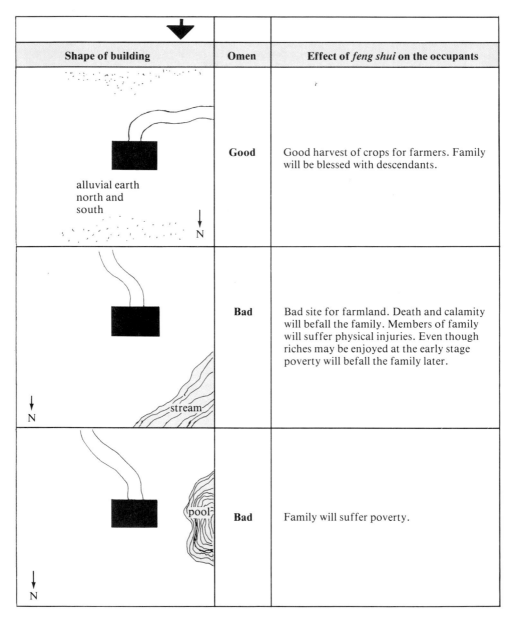

Shape of building	Omen	Effect of *feng shui* on the occupants
alluvial earth north and south	Good	Good harvest of crops for farmers. Family will be blessed with descendants.
stream	Bad	Bad site for farmland. Death and calamity will befall the family. Members of family will suffer physical injuries. Even though riches may be enjoyed at the early stage poverty will befall the family later.
pool	Bad	Family will suffer poverty.

The following photographs of models, depicting the good or bad layout of building blocks are derived from the *Yang Zhai Shi Shu* (阻宅十书).

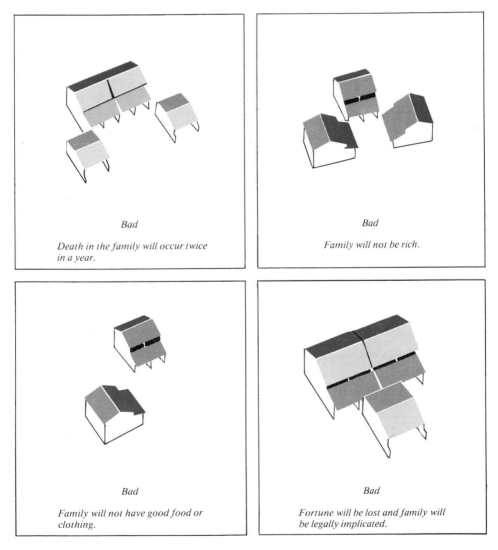

Bad

Death in the family will occur twice in a year.

Bad

Family will not be rich.

Bad

Family will not have good food or clothing.

Bad

Fortune will be lost and family will be legally implicated.

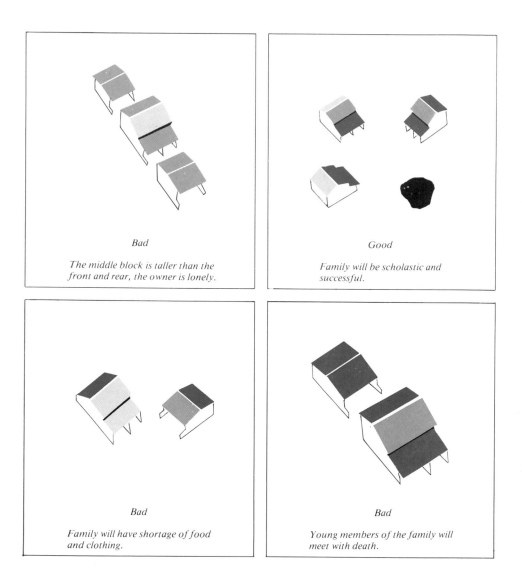

Bad

The middle block is taller than the front and rear, the owner is lonely.

Good

Family will be scholastic and successful.

Bad

Family will have shortage of food and clothing.

Bad

Young members of the family will meet with death.

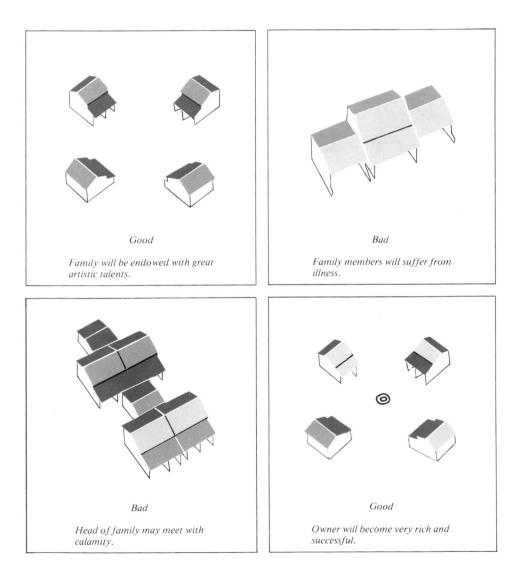

Good

Family will be endowed with great artistic talents.

Bad

Family members will suffer from illness.

Bad

Head of family may meet with calamity.

Good

Owner will become very rich and successful.

The following situations regarded as being unfavourable are given in the *Water Dragon Classic* (600 A.D.) The dot represents the house while the lines are water courses.

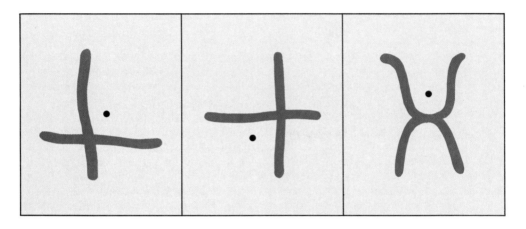

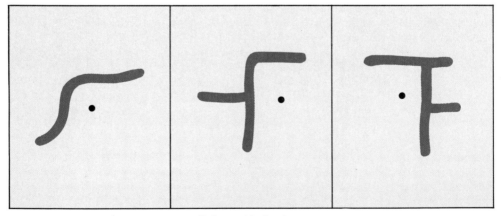

Unfavourable situations

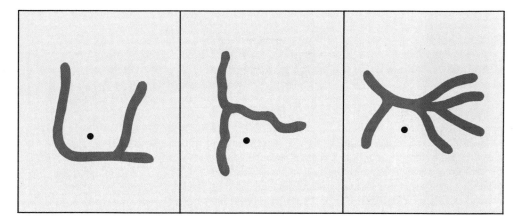

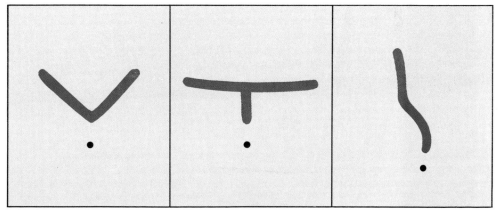

Unfavourable situations

The following diagrams are also derived from the *Water Dragon Classic*. The dot represents the house while the lines represent the water courses.

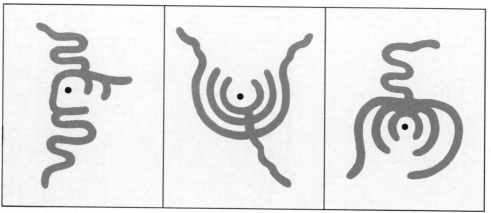

Site of posterity,
wealth and fame

Site of good fortune

Site of posterity and wealth

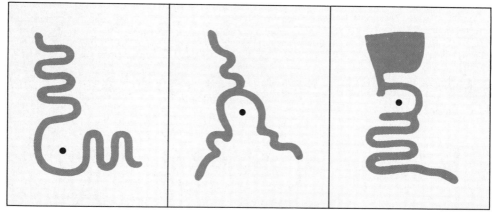

Site of posterity,
fame and fortune

Site of wealth and
prosperous well-being

Site of posterity and wealth

Favourable situations

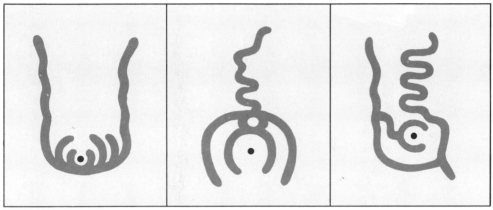

Site of great wealth and posterity

Site of posterity and wealth

Site of posterity

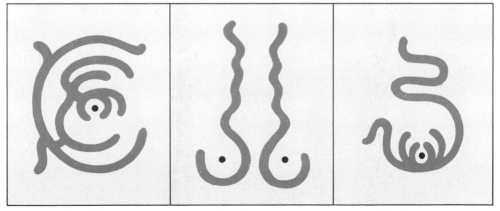

Site of fame

Site of greatness

Site of posterity, fame and fortune

Favourable situations

一九七九年二月夢霞

7 Examples of Buildings Influenced by *Feng Shui*

Forlag's *Chinese Buddhist Monasteries*[1] gives numerous examples of Chinese temples in China under the influence of *feng shui*. He says that for centuries *feng shui* played and still plays an important part in the building history of monasteries.

In Singapore the fact that geomancy has been considered an important factor for the choice of a site is evident in a few temples as it is clearly carved on the stone plaques. For example, neatly carved on a stone plaque, dated 1887, in the Giok Hong Tian (玉皇殿), Havelock Road, Singapore, is the following:

爱思作庙卜基於永全街中，背山环港，渊涵岳峙，绕缘送青胜地也，且与前所自建之真君庙相去仅数十武耳，而后光辉映具有胜地也。

Briefly it means that the temple was built at a "peaceful and wholesome street", with the hill at its back and the Singapore River in front. The surrounding area was greenery and the site was indeed a good piece of land. Besides, it was very near to the Cheng Yuen Chang Kuan temple which Hong Lim built.

Plaque at Giok Hong Tian, Singapore ▲

[1] Forlag, *Chinese Buddhist Monasteries,* London, 1937.

The Guan Yin Tong (观音堂) at Telok Blangah Drive, Singapore, is another excellent example of a Chinese temple with good *feng shui*. Built in 1886, it is situated on high ground overlooking the sea, benefiting from the *yang* of the lower vacant land at the front. It is protected on the sides and at the back by hilly ground in accordance with the Chinese saying *zuo san wang hai* (坐山望海), i.e. ''sitting on the hill and overlooking the sea''.

◀ *Guan Yin Tong today with high-rise flats in the background.*

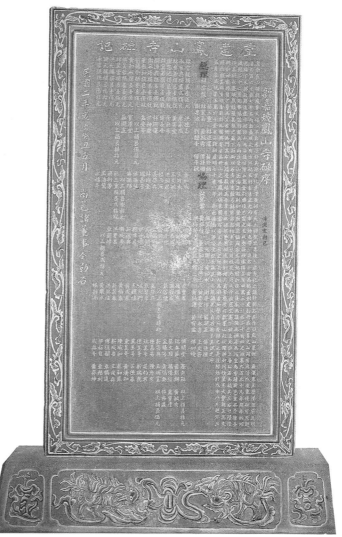

▲ *The stone plaque at Hong San Temple also testifies that the temple was built on a site chosen for its excellent geomantic qualities.*

▲ *Guan Yin Tong as it was in 1880. The photograph was taken by the temple's caretaker Mr Lee.*

▲ *Wak Hai Cheng Bio, Singapore*

The Wak Hai Cheng Bio (粤海清庙), a Chinese temple built in 1852 on Philip Street, Singapore, was designed (according to the *luopan*) to orientate towards *yi* with its rear facing *xin* for the concentration of beneficial influences. Before the siting of the temple was finalized the high ground and low area around it were studied. The principal clues of the whereabouts of cosmic breath were captured and the water sources and courses were ob-

served before the location and orientation of the temple were established. The interesting and intricate decorative motifs and ceramic symbols employed on the roof and the walls of the temple signify the sense of authority, the blessings of the gods and protection from evil influences. Its azure dragon on the left wall and the white tiger on the right are symbolic of the life-giving ''breaths'' of nature.

The Kek Lok See (极乐寺), Penang, the largest and most well-known Chinese temple in Malaysia, is on a hill which looks like a flying stork, a bird associated with longevity in Chinese myths and symbolism. The *feng shui* of the site seems perfect as the Dragon Hill is on its left while the White Elephant Hill is on its right. Numerous temple sites were originally chosen for their geomantic qualities. The Sam Poh Tong Temple (三保洞) at Ipoh, Malaysia, is a good example. It appears that the cave formation resembles a dragon with its head near the entrance and its tail opening into an air-well at the rear. The air-well is about seventy metres in diameter and is surrounded by steep rock terraces which rise to a height of about thirty-three metres making a strikingly strong contrast to the low, dark tail of the open air-well. It is highly desirable to have the dragon in the cave as China's three great primary "dragons" have their origin in the mountains of Central Asia.[1]

Some commercial buildings, temples, office blocks and hotels in Singapore and Malaysia have been subjected to the computation of *feng shui* rules. A few of them are illustrated here.

1

[1] The "dragon" is a beneficent force which animates the hills. It is a *yang* force which dwells in the eastern quarters of the heavens.

2

1   *A shophouse with red banners and a flag of the Eight Trigrams.*

2   *A town house with a flag printed with a pattern of the Eight Trigrams.*

3   *A shophouse with the sign of the Eight Trigrams above the door.*

▲ *The former Nanyang University. The undulating ground is the true profile of the dragon. The buildings have the hills as a backing and the pond at the front. The site has excellent geomantic values.*

An institution of higher studies, the former Nanyang University in Singapore, was sited geomantically well on a piece of interesting, undulating land with smooth physical features that are in accordance with nature and beneficial influences. The surrounding landscape is indicative of balanced patterns and harmonious topography. Ranges of hilly ground spread on the left (resembling the formation of the azure dragon and the *yang* energy),

while slightly lower hilly areas run along the right (the white tiger and the *yin* force). Where these two energies converge, the land formation resembles a horseshoe which is bounded at its open tips by a meandering stream. The campus was planned on a *zi-wu* (north/south) direction or axis according to the *luopan*.

Hong San Temple ▶

Ridge detail of Hong San Temple showing
▼ *Guan Di on a hip.*

Raised above the general ground level for about nine metres the Hong San Temple has a commanding view of the surrounding area and the sea. Its *feng shui* is said to be good as it has the hill at its back and the sea in front.

The planning concept and decorative style of the temple are of Chinese palace fashion. As can be seen the ridges have graceful curves and ornaments. The ornaments on the eaves are richly carved and gilt. The pillars have the dragons entwined, signifying the power and prestige of palatial structures.

Facade of Hong San Temple. Notice the encircled hu lu *in the centre of the ridge.* Hu lu *is a kind of gourd found in China, supposed to have been used by one of the eight Immortals to carry wine.*

The ridge decorations of the temple are typical of the Nam Ann style. (Nam Ann is a province in China.) At the centre of the ridge is a *hu lu* (胡芦) shown in a magical ring of fire. At the terminals of the upturned ridge are the ceramic dancing dragons, symbolizing the vigour and power of the gods. On the sides of the ridge piece are ceramic frescoes of dragons, chimeras (mythical quadrupeds resembling lions), dragon fishes, phoenixes and lions, signifying blessings and good omens. The hips of the ridge terminate in statues of ceramic artifacts of the god of war (Guan Di) on the right and the warrior Xi Ma on the left. The gods of luck and prosperity are also portrayed on the hips. The reddish roof tiles signify joy and they terminate in green-edged tiles which have the colour of jade symbolizing rejuvenation and an evergreen quality.

Another example of an interesting roof design is the ridge of the Giok Hong Tian. Here the ridge decoration of the main shrine is elaborate. Dancing dragons of ceramic flank the magical celestial blazing pearl at the centre. (Among roof ornaments for warding off evil influences and bringing beneficial forces, the theme expressing dancing dragons flanking the celestial pearl seems to be the most common for temple buildings.) The ridge piece in concrete is decorated with ceramic compositions of flowers, plants and birds of good omen. The tilted ridges terminate in spirals while the roof hips terminate in figurines representing the gods of sun, wind, rain and thunder.

Examples of Buildings Influenced by Feng Shui

◀ *Ridge of the Giok Hong Tian. The fish dragons on the main ridge are symbolic of success and the gods of sun, wind, rain and thunder on the hips are protectors against calamities.*

▼ *Thian Hock Keng Temple, Singapore. Both the main shrine hall and the entrance area have dancing dragons flanking the blazing pearl.*

Geomantic objects or carvings such as a magical red cloth, or dancing dragons or the Eight Trigrams are often used on the main ridge ceiling beams of buildings. Such objects can be found in the ridge beams of the Leong San See and Ho Lum Kong.

The mythical guardians of good report are symbolized by the white tiger of the west (or right) and the azure dragon of the east (or left). They can also be represented by the words *loong yin* (龙吟) or "dragon speaks" on the left and *hu xiao* (虎啸) or "tiger roars" on the right. The white tiger is always placed at the right side of a building or temple and the azure dragon is always placed on the left. Legend has it that the white tiger was the son of a courtier of the tyrant Chou Wang of the Yuan dynasty. The courtier was murdered by Chou Wang's aides. In trying to avenge his father's murder the son was killed. He was later canonized as the spirit of the white tiger star. The azure dragon was one of the chief generals of the last emperor of the Yuan dynasty. He was made a prisoner of war, executed and later deified as the azure dragon star.

◄ *The Wak Hai Cheng Bio is one of the oldest temples in Singapore. Built in the early nineteenth century, it has the most complicated and ornate roof decorations. The mini-structures that resemble a miniature Chinese town and Chinese figurines possibly signify joy, activity and happiness.*

▼ *Ceiling of Ho Lum Kong showing a red cloth with the Eight Trigrams or* bagua.

1

2

1 *In broken porcelain pieces stuck onto a painted red rectangle above the side door of the Tung Shan Tong are the words* loong yin *significant of the azure dragon which wards off evil influences.*

2 *Trusses of Wak Hai Cheng Bio, with carvings and symbols of good omen.*

3   *In the Tung Shan Tong,* opposite loong yin *is* hu xiao *meaning "tiger roars", symbolic of the white tiger which is a guardian against wandering spirits.*

4   *Ridge beam of the Guan Yin Tong. The Eight Trigrams and patterns of good omen were painted on the ridge beam when the structure was first erected. The patterns beautifully carved in gold are geomantic symbols to render protection against evil spirits.*

▲ *Moulded on the wall of the Wak Hai Cheng Bio, just below a small air-well, the "white tiger" guards the temple against evil influences.*

▲ *The azure dragons of the Wak Hai Cheng Bio, dancing with vigour and spirit, are symbolic of the power they possess against evil spirits.*

▼ *Ridge beams of Leong San See. The main ridge beam has two dancing dragons and a celestial pearl carved and coated in gold to symbolize power and to render geomantic value to the building.*

▲ Yin *and* yang *are sometimes identified with the green or azure dragon and the white tiger. The pictures above and on pages 100 and 101 depict the dragon and tiger at the main prayer hall of the Leong San See. In this instance, however, both are painted brown.*

Feng shui is not only practised in China, Singapore and Malaysia but also in Hong Kong, Taiwan and Japan. *The Asia Magazine* of 1 May 1977 gave one example. When the government of Hong Kong set out to build low-cost housing for the people, there was more than just buildings to be considered—centuries of religion and superstitions had to be taken into account as well. *Feng shui* still exists as a spiritual compass in the minds of the older and rural Chinese. Presently *feng shui* is tacitly considered by engineers and architects of Hong Kong's Public Works Department. It is interesting to note *The Asia Magazine's* report on the reconstruction of Sham Tseng village in

▼ *Ridge beam of Leong San See showing a red cloth placed on the main ridge as a good omen.*

Hong Kong. Objections and complaints were made to the architect when one block of houses was sited on a line parallel to an access road. The architect eventually had to solve the problem of *feng shui* by moving the building line a degree or two. When one of the houses on the tip of the arc arrangement was sited beyond the protective shelter of the hill, objections from the villagers were once again raised. To pacify the people the architect had to propose a wall three metres high along the crest of the hill and along-side the exposed houses to act as shelter against the wind and evil forces.

Choosing a location and an auspicious opening date for business premises through a *feng shui* expert is practically mandatory in Hong Kong. The *New Nation* of 19 July 1978 reported an interesting incident. It appears that Chase Asia Ltd., Chase Manhattan's merchant bank in Hong Kong, lost four big business deals in a row. As a result an expert on *feng shui* was consulted. Business has improved tremendously since the implementation of *feng shui* remedial actions.

▲ *The boat in a restaurant in Hyatt Hotel, Singapore was built in accordance with a geomancer's instructions and used to store raw seafood. It symbolizes "plain sailing" and is*

Geomancy practices also flourish widely in Taiwan. It was reported in *The Asia Magazine* (7 October 1973) that there were between 20,000 and 30,000 geomancers in Taiwan. The report said that the Lo brothers (obviously a prominent family in Taiwan) are rich and their eight sons have obtained doctorial degrees because the *feng shui* of the Lo family land is auspicious. Another vivid example was given. A few years ago, a certain doctor in Taipei was puzzled by the fact that a patient had recurrent attacks of tuberculosis.

supposed to bring good business to the restaurant. The photograph is misleading as it appears that there are two boats, but note the single roof and the linking net.

Unable to cope with his patient's ailment, the doctor advised him to seek help from a geomancer. A well-known *feng shui* expert, Mr Tang Cheng-yi, was consulted. Mr Tang visited the sick man's house and felt the presence of a "killing spirit". Using the geomancer's compass, he proposed an alternative entrance and closed the front gate. The man recovered speedily from his illness and since then has suffered no recurrence of tuberculosis.

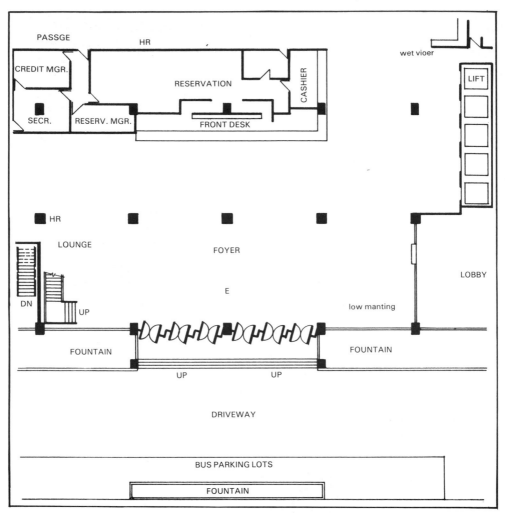

▲ *Ground floor plan of Hyatt Hotel, Singapore.*

One of the fountains in front of Hyatt Hotel. The fountains have to be ▶
maintained at a certain height to bring prosperity.

A site with good geomancy can be ruined by interference from undesirable
geomantic elements. It naturally follows that it can be enhanced by improve-
ments. The widely known Hyatt Hotel in Singapore is an excellent example.
It appears that the hotel's business progressed tremendously after the con-
sultation of a well-known geomancer. Originally the entrance doors to the
foyer were parallel to the main road. The cashier's desk was also parallel
to the door and road.

▲ *Hyatt Hotel (doors)*

According to geomantic theory, in such a situation wealth would flow out of the hotel easily. Also the undesirable spirits could enter without difficulty as the doors faced northwest. When the geomancer was called upon to improve the *feng shui* of the hotel he recommended altering the main doors and had them built at an angle to the road as shown in the plan. In this way wealth could be retained and the evil influences, if any, would be trapped at the awkward corners of the doors. The geomancer also recommended the removal of the fountains directly in front of the hotel and had them replaced

by flower beds. A flag pole, also in front of the hotel, was removed to the fourth floor and two new fountains were built at auspicious places on either side of the main doors. A Chinese boat to signify the "safe voyage" of the business venture was made and placed in the restaurant on the first floor. Besides these minor alterations to improve the *feng shui* of the hotel, prayers were offered and the blessings of heaven and earth were called upon to bring prosperity and good business to the hotel management.

8 Structures or Objects to Remedy Geomantic Defects

The physical universe is alive with forces of *yin* and *yang*. These forces can be formed in harmony or converge to interact vigorously so as to bear fruit for a dwelling and its occupants. Conversely should the male and female energies be deemed to be in discord, evil influences would prevail and modifications to the landscape or structures would be necessary to bring upon a new balance of beneficial forces.

The ancient Chinese had various structures or objects to remedy geomantic defects. The most common and popular structure was the pagoda. Practically every town in China has at least one pagoda. According to William Willets the city of Ch'uan-Chou was shaped like a carp (the carp is a good shape in geomancy) but its good *feng shui* was disturbed by a neighbouring town which was in the form of a fishing net![1] The inhabitants of Ch'uan Chou remedied the geomantic defect by building two tall pagodas to intercept the net. From this example it can be concluded that the Chinese believed that geomantic defects could be remedied by the construction of pagodas and that the *feng shui* of a dwelling or a town could be influenced by neighbouring dwellings or towns. On the other hand, should the *feng shui* of a place be good, harmony would prevail as long as that *status quo* was maintained. *The Asia Magazine* (May 1977) reported that when engineers decided to modernize communications between Hong Kong and Canton and hoist the first telegraph pole, objections from *feng shui* believers were voiced. According to the report, Canton was "the city of the rams" and in the careful balance of opposing forces it was guarded by the tiger's mouth and the nine dragons of Kowloon. If the rams were led by a string (the telegraph line) through the nine dragons, i.e. Kowloon, disaster would prevail.

Should a building be badly designed geomantically or the site be subjected to evil influences as a result of the conflicting conjunctions of cosmological or astrological bodies, the beneficial *qi* or cosmic breath would be turned into *sha qi* (煞气) or breath of ill-fortune. *Sha qi* is said to travel in straight lines and it can be "deflected" by a screen, a fence, an embankment, a mirror or an object or charm, e.g. the Eight Trigrams with a mirror in the centre.

---

[1] William Willets, *Chinese Art,* 2 Vols., Penguin, London, 1958.

▲ *Model of a five-tiered pagoda, made by the author.*

▲ *Residential house with the Eight Trigrams hung above the antique main door.*

▲
*This town house accommodates a few families.
Note that the Eight Trigrams above a window
on the second floor is used to ward off evil
influences while a mirror is placed above a
window on the first floor to deflect bad luck.
The practice of using mirrors to deflect the
path of malevolent spirits is also popular in
Hong Kong.* The Asia Magazine *(May 1977)
reports that the colony is full of houses with
mirrors facing some line of approach of
malevolent spirits.*

Residential house with the Eight Trigrams ▶
surrounding a mirror.

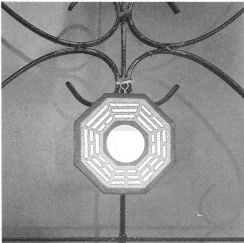

▲ *The Eight Trigrams cast on a concrete slab measuring almost 1½ metres square. Notice the* yin-yang *symbol of black and white like two fish, head to tail, at the centre.*

◀ *The pattern of the Eight Trigrams is also used on buildings and on tables to reflect* sha qi *and to bring good fortune. The photograph shows such a pattern on a screen at the Guan Yin Tong.*

9 Some Thoughts on Geomantic Colours

It has been explained earlier that the northeast is occupied by the fearful "dark" or evil spirits. The south, which has an auspicious disposition, is associated with red, an emblem of joy and festivity. Related to the fire of the Five Elements, red is used to paint the door gods to ward off all evil influences. Reflecting the *yang* principle, red is a symbol of virtue and sincerity. Yellow that was once the national and royal colour of the Chinese is now used for garments of Taoist priests, for burying the dead and for geomantic blessings. Charms against the fearful dark corridors of evil influences are written on yellow paper. Emblematic of the earth, yellow denotes the *yin* principle. Green is related to wood whose foliage evokes the energy of potent growth, youthfulness, posterity and harmony with other colours. It is the colour of the dragon of the east in geomantic terms.

White is a colour of autumn. It is emblematic of the element metal and is related to the west orientation. It is also representative of purity. Finally, black is the north, winter and the element of water. It denotes the consequence of man, death, mourning and penance. Metaphysically it is the colour of calamity, guilt and evil influences.

▼ *A shop in Singapore completely painted red.*

▲ *Green is related to wood whose foliage evokes the energy of potent growth, youthfulness and prosperity. For good* feng shui *it is often used on glazed porcelain "bamboo" grilles or on tiles of temple roofs.*

1

1   *Bracketing system of Hong San Temple in Singapore. Note that green is painted on the ceiling as a sign of longevity.*

2   *Red is related to fire and is applied to doors or buildings to symbolize heavenly blessings and happiness. The gates of Wak Hai Cheng Bio are painted with the pattern of the bats signifying luck, blessing and joy.*

▼ *Cobalt blue, the colour of heaven, contrasts vividly with the auspicious red of the carved door panels.*

▲ *Yellow or gold — geomantically speaking the colour of the Mandate of Heaven, but to Buddhists, Nirvana—is used to contrast with brilliant red to add richness to this extremely intricate and complicated bracketing system of Thian Hock Keng Temple in Singapore.*

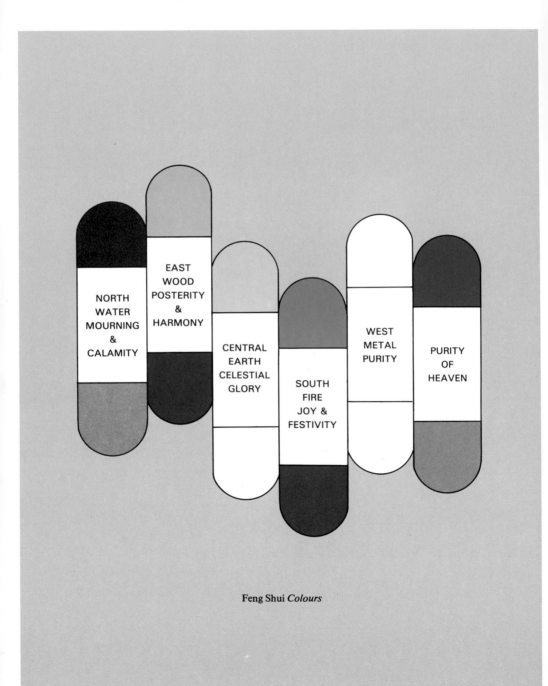

Feng Shui *Colours*

Glossary

Azure dragon (青龍)	One of the mythical guardians of good reports, always placed on the left of a building.
Bagua (八卦)	The Eight Trigrams.
Bing (丙)	One of the Ten Stems, meaning "the root of growth".
Chen (辰)	One of the Twelve Branches, meaning "progress".
Chinese Animal Year	Each lunar year is represented by an animal symbol in the following order: dragon, snake, horse, goat, monkey, cock, dog, pig, rat, bull, tiger and rabbit.
Chou (丑)	One of the Twelve Branches, meaning "the growth".
Cosmic breath	The breath of life for the dead which the Chinese believe essential for the well-being of the buried.
Di-ji jia (地理家)	*Di-li* means geography while *di-li jia* means a specialist who divinates the future by observing the geographical features of a site.
Ding (丁)	One of the Ten Stems, meaning "maturity".
Double hours	The Chinese give each period of duration of two hours a name, e.g. *Chou* (丑) is from 1 a.m. to 3 a.m. and *Yin* (寅) from 3 a.m. to 5 a.m.
Eight Trigrams (八卦)	Its original form is attributed to Fu-Hsi (2852 B.C.); it indicates the eight points of the compass.
Feng shui (風水)	Geomancy — the words mean "wind and water". Actually they define the geographical features of the area in which a tomb or a building is situated.
Five Elements (五行)	Conceived as the five forces of nature by the Chinese as early as the 4th century B.C. and designed in the sequence: gold or metal, wood, water, fire and earth.
Geng (庚)	One of the Ten Stems, meaning "fullness leading to change".
Geomancer	One who specialises in the art of divining the future from the geographical or orientational features of a tomb or a building.
Giok Hong Tian (玉皇殿)	A Chinese temple at Havelock Road, Singapore.
Guan Di (關帝)	God of War, a great warrior of the "Three Kingdom" period.
Guan Yin Tong (觀音堂)	A Chinese temple at Telok Blangah Drive, Singapore.
Hai (亥)	One of the Twelve Branches, meaning "nucleus".

Hong San Temple (鳳山寺)	A Chinese temple at Mohd. Sultan Road, Singapore.
Hu lu (葫蘆)	A magical object which is supposed to have been shaped and fashioned after a fruit found in China and is believed to be able to capture evil spirits.
Hyatt	A well-known hotel at Scotts Road, Singapore.
Ji	One of the Ten Stems, meaning "liberation".
Jia	One of the Ten Stems, meaning "the sign of growth".
Kan-yu jia (堪輿家)	*Feng shui* specialist.
Kui (癸)	One of the Ten Stems, meaning "the preparation for spring".
Lao Zi (老子)	An older contemporary of Confucius (551 — 497 B.C.); he founded Taoism which advocates "conformity" to the way of the Universe.
Leong San See (龍山寺)	A Chinese temple at Race Course Road, Singapore.
Long (龍)	Dragon, a symbol of the beneficial forces of nature, representing the topography of the site.
Luopan (羅盤)	Geomancer's compass, an instrument for the divination and orientation of buildings and tombstones.
Mao (卯)	One of the Twelve Branches, meaning "fullness".
Ren (壬)	One of the Ten Stems, meaning "the height of function".
Sha (砂)	Means "sand"; in geomancy it represents the environment of the site.
Sha qi (煞氣)	"Breath that hurts", meaning "evil influence prevails".
Shen (申)	One of the Twelve Branches, meaning "the expanded form of maturity".
Shu (戌)	One of the Twelve Branches, meaning "death".
Shui (水)	Means "water" and it symbolizes the streams flowing through the site.
Si (巳)	One of the Twelve Branches, meaning "renewed".
Song of Geomancy	Sometimes known as the *Book of Burial*, written in twenty parts by Kuo P'u during the 4th century B.C.

Tai Ji (太極)	"The Great Extreme".
Tai Yang (太陽)	The sun
Tai Yin (太陰)	The moon
Ten Stems (天干)	Also known as *Tian Gan,* a term introduced by the Chinese before 1766 B.C. for things related to Heaven.
Thian Hock Kong (天福宮)	A Chinese temple at Telok Ayer Street, Singapore.
Tong Shu (通書)	Chinese annual almanac.
Twelve Branches (地支)	Also known as *Di Zhi,* a term introduced by the Chinese before 1766 B.C. for things related to the Earth.
Wak Hai Cheng Bio (粵海清廟)	A Chinese temple at Philip Street, Singapore.
Wei (未)	One of the Twelve Branches, meaning "smell of matured objects".
White Tiger (白虎)	One of the mythical guardians of good report, always placed on the right side of a building.
Wu (戊)	One of the Ten Stems, meaning "a stage of fullness in growth".
Xiang (向)	The orientation of a tomb or building in *feng shui* assessment.
Xin (辛)	One of the Ten Stems, meaning "restoration".
Xue (穴)	Means a hole, but in geomancy it represents the foundation of a tomb or building.
Yi (乙)	One of the Ten Stems, meaning "the spread of growth".
Yi-Jing (易經)	The *Book of Changes,* a book of prophecies based on the principles of *yin* and *yang.*
Yin (寅)	One of the Twelve Branches, meaning "spreading the growth".
Yin-yang (陰陽)	The negative and positive principles of things in the Universe. *Yang* is bright, masculine and powerful, while *yin* is dark, feminine and absorbent.
You (酉)	One of the Twelve Branches, meaning "ripeness".
Zhui Zi (諸子)	A famous Taoist during 300 B.C.
Zhu Yuan Zhang (朱元璋)	First Emperor of the Ming Dynasty.
Zi (子)	One of the Twelve Branches, meaning "young shoot of a plant".

Other books on Chinese subjects published by
Times Books International:

Feng Shui for the Home, by Evelyn Lip. A companion guide to *Chinese Geomancy*, essential for those who wish to locate, channel and benefit from the *qi* or cosmic breath in their homes, apartments, shops and offices.

Chinese Temples and Deities, by Evelyn Lip. A fully illustrated authoritative study of the constructional styles of some well known temples in China and Southeast Asia.

Chinese Crafts, by Roberta Helmer Stalberg and Ruth Nesi. A highly readable guide to the magnificent ceramic, lacquer, bronze, silk, ivory and jade crafts of China.

Straits Chinese Silver, by Ho Wing Meng. A beautifully illustrated collector's guide to this unusual cross-cultural art form.

Straits Chinese Porcelain, by Ho Wing Meng. A comprehensive look into this unique form of functional, decorative art.

Straits Chinese Beadwork and Embroidery, by Ho Wing Meng. A highly informative illustrated description of the origins and use of beadwork and embroidery in the cultural heritage of the Babas and Nonyas.

Your Chinese Roots, by Thomas Tan Tsu Wee. A book of origins which delves into the patterns of Chinese emigration and the principles which keep these far-flung communities intact.